THE GREAT
MYSTERY

A Theological Study of the Trinity

Jason Hoke

Table of Contents

ACKNOWLEDGEMENT

Although this assignment is a little over the ten pages I was assigned back in 1995, I set out to do justice to the study of the Trinity. What started as a spring break project has turned into a study that I can say, I now know a lot more and a lot less about the Trinity than when I started. This is just the beginning of knowing and loving God. These 120 plus pages will no doubt grow as my studies continue in the future. In the final reading for this project, I came across two to three more resources to add later.

I wish to thank Dr. Barry Morgan for setting the bar high. Even though the computer ate my first paper, and I did not have a passing paper following the second attempt, I wish to stay disciplined and continue the journey of knowing God more. I also wish to thank the Doctors Bergen for inviting me to campus last spring to speak to the students in Christian Ministry Vocation Fellowship. It was here that I challenged the students to never stop learning, and in the process I was challenged to do this project for myself.

Lastly, I wish to thank my family. For a year and a half I have had notecards spread out everywhere. I thank you and Parker Lee for reading this paper for grammar and clarification. Any mistakes are all my own. Thank you, Dr. Phil Bray, for reading it over and encouraging me in this project.

Jason Hoke

DEDICATION

Dedicated to my wife Belinda and our children Caleb and Sarah.
God has greatly blessed us, even in the hard times of health.

INTRODUCTION

The study of the Trinity is a very complex endeavor that will never truly be understood by the created man. However, God is relational and desires to know his creation intimately. In His pursuit of knowing mankind, He has given tools for man to know, love, worship, and honor Him on a personal level. Just as a husband may never fully understand his wife, however, he will forever try to know her more each day, so we must look deep into our relationship with our creator.1 All healthy relationships have functioning two-way communication. It must become the desire of the creation to reciprocate the loving action of the Creator. A husband must show selfless affection toward his wife, and the wife must return that affection for a healthy relationship to grow. The act of love will then develop deeper affections, like trust. There are no exceptions in the God-to-man relationship. The biggest difference in the development of a God-to-man relationship is that God must be the initiator of this relationship. God came to man first in the garden, and it is God who initiates a love that can only be given back once it has been experienced. 1 John 4:19 tells the reader that man loves because God "first loved us." This study will be discussed in a later chapter, but man must know that to be loved is to be known, and God is the instigator of that love. The study of the Trinity has not always been a heavily debated subject due to the overall agreement among scholars throughout the years. However, there have been four very controversial centuries with great debates concerning the teachings on

---

1.Timothy and Denise George, Ed, *Baptist Confessions, Covenants, and Catechisms*. (Nashville: B&H Books, 1996), 44.

the Trinity, those being the 4th, 19th, 20th, and 21st centuries. It became such an issue at those times that church councils were called to help with stopping heresies that arose out of the unorthodox views of some of the church leaders, starting in the 4th century. During the other seventeen centuries of Christianity, the Trinity was considered a benign topic with little interest for debate. Very few scholars had been open to debating the topic for hundreds of years. This theological understanding is one of the main foundations of Christianity. This doctrine is very much like the nerve center of the human body. Once you begin by defining one concept, all the other parts must fit for it to work. If a man were to have a sore on his foot, he might take a short step with the hurt foot and a regular step with the good foot. This compensation would help with the immediate pain. However, after three months of not having the foot healed, the man now has a sore hip. Two weeks later, he has a sore back, and he is walking with a limp. This pain then goes to his neck and shoulders. Eventually, the man can no longer walk at all, and his whole body is affected. Much is the same with the Trinity. Once you overemphasize or compensate for a wrong doctrine or assumption of belief, you lose the ability to function as a Church, and your view of God is incorrect. It is of great relief that the debates on the Trinity were at a minimum in most of church history. It is also the view here that God has preserved our understanding of who He is so that the church would prevail.

No matter what century, man has continuously tried to understand his Creator more. In this endeavor, it has been discovered that attempting to understand an infinite being with a finite mind leads to false understandings. This makes it hard to ensure false understandings are kept in check. Every person doing an investigation comes into their investigation with preconceived notions on the subject, which will affect their overall view. When misunderstandings or incorrect presuppositions appear, they will lead scholars to false conclusions. People from around the world and from different religious backgrounds think deeply about the concept of who God is and how He has revealed Himself to His people. This possibility should not stop us from doing all that is possible to know the great Creator. No other doctrinal study seems as difficult as the Trinity due to its inherent complexity. The doctrine of the Trinity is one of the greatest mysteries of the church age. The Trinity is often inappropriately called a contradiction by those who oppose Christianity, but that mystery, though not yet revealed, can be understood.2 It is the intent of this book to let the Bible speak for itself with as little personal input as possible. While examining key passages there will be an introduction of monotheism, an investigation into the claims of deity from the Father, Son, and Holy Spirit, an overview consulting key historical moments in the church and its councils, and a final discovery of the three main Persons of the Godhead and their relation to one another, yet remaining a mystery and not a contradiction.

The first concept to be seen is one found throughout the Bible. There are three "Persons" claiming deity, yet God calls Himself "one" in Deuteronomy 6. God the Father is seen as the predominant figure throughout the Old Testament. He is defined as "Father" by Jesus in the New Testament. Outside of the specific occasions where the Spirit of God is used in the Old Testament, the reference would be to the Father. Jesus, the Son, is seen as having equality with the Father in the New Testament, and the Holy Spirit is also recognized as a deity in both the New and Old Testaments. The question for the Christian must be answered: how can God be monotheistic and yet have three persons claiming deity? God is a mystery, but He has given His finite people enough clues to understand who He is and how He functions. Even at this stage in the investigation, many Christians throw up their hands and say the Trinity is too complicated, or it does not matter. To

---

2 R.C. Sproul, Mystery of the Trinity, http://www.ligonier.org/learn/series/
mystery-of-the-trinity/ (accessed March 22, 2016).

abdicate our responsibility of understanding God and letting the religious leaders of our time decide personal beliefs will inevitably lead to false teachings and heresy. It is this author's opinion that Christians are not to give over their beliefs to any man outside of Christ. Many just follow church leaders because it is easy. This can lead to easy-believism. This is where people accept what an authority figure tells them as the easy way to accomplish a spiritual task. For instance, a pastor might say God is love and loves all people just the way they are. This leads the congregation to stop calling for repentance because, if God can accept people into heaven as they are, then why repent? It then becomes obvious that those who follow have abandoned verification through self-study. The people need to see that God does love all people, but He is also holy and just. In today's world, we see that salvation has taken on incorrect definitions because pastors have a misconception of the Trinity and our need for Lordship as a part of the salvation experience, and the people blindly follow. According to Albert Mohler, "the good news of Christ has given way to the bad news of an insidious easy-believism that makes no moral demands on the lives of sinners."[3] This is much like a person who wishes to build a new house. The first step after owning the property is laying out the foundation. Most homeowners at this point in the construction need help in the actual formation of the foundation. The owner can simply look up information on a contractor, have the job bid, and pay the deposit no questions asked. The owner might be a bit more inquisitive and ask for three bids from different contractors, believing that if they have a business, they know what they are talking about. The wise owner puts in the work needed for a good foundation. He knows the county codes. He asks what the concrete mix ratios will be. He then asks what kind of reinforcements will be used. He will

---

3 Albert Mohler, albertmohler.com: The Gospel According to Jesus-20 years later, (albertmohler.com articles June 2, 2008) accessed November 11, 2022.

probably get several references and secure insurance and bonds from the company before proceeding. This can all seem like overkill. Most of the time, everything will work out just fine, but when you are dealing with a foundation, you are dealing with the rest of the house. If a paint color is wrong, it is easy to fix. If the toilet needs fixing, it is difficult and time-consuming to fix, but if the foundation is off, the only option might be to tear down the whole house and start over. Our relationship with God is much like having a good foundation of our faith. If you do not put in the time and proper effort with God, you have failed, and the foundation of your relationship will crumble. You might assume the rest will be fine, but if you are trusting in a pastor to feed you the information about your eternal destiny and do not check it out yourself, there will be only one person to blame: yourself. Our relationship with God is the foundation of all other beliefs and must be treated as extremely important. The Trinity has to hold to a very tight line of factual assumptions gathered from the Scriptures, and these beliefs need to be practiced by the adherents. One overreach to one side or the other will swiftly lead to a bad practice and eventually heresy.

The ultimate focus of any relationship that leads to our doctrinal beliefs must first concentrate on the original source. This source is what we turn to in order to secure our understanding of truth and direction. It would not matter if every theologian and scholar throughout history agreed on an issue if they did not have the Bible to give them direction concerning the Trinity. It is here that the establishment of the Bible as the original source is a founding presupposition. This statement alone would cause at least a third of the Christian world to recoil because they would hold that the history of the church is on equal footing to Scripture. The Roman Catholic Church is the largest Christian denomination, and as a body, it would not agree with *Sola Scriptura*. They would place church history, church teaching, and the Bible on equal footing.[4] They would even place the church teachings over the Bible since it was the church that determined what books were considered canon[5]. However, this study will examine the characteristics of what God has to say about Himself in the Bible as the primary source. This book will use the *Sola Scriptura* as not only a presupposition, but it will help demonstrate that the Bible alone should be the rule in church history and church dogma, and never the other way around. It is with great effort that the texts will be exegeted and that the meaning will only come from the text, not from the author's presuppositions. It is far too easy to hold a sacred belief and then find the texts that seem to help substantiate the belief, rather than studying a set of texts and letting it determine our beliefs.

With this established, it is asked, who does He say he is? It is important to remember, "Because God is infinite and we are finite, we will never fully understand God."[6] God shows us that knowing Him is possible and should be pursued. He does this by giving us hints into His being. Now it is time for us to discover what He has already established and build from there.

The philosophical argument for essence versus existence will be discussed more in-depth later, but one must see that Scripture is clear when it tells us, "Long ago, You established the earth, and the heavens are the work of your hands. They will perish, but you will endure. . . . But you are the same, and your years will never end." [7] To know Him, we must know the presuppositions of any argument. The start of this study will begin with a presupposition: the Bible shows us that

---

4 George, 159.
5 Millard J Erickson, Christian Theology: Thrid edition, (Grand Rapids: Baker Books, 2013), 216.
6 Wayne Grudem. Systematic Theology. (Grand Rapids: Zondervan, 1994), 149.
7 Ps. 102:25-27(HCSB).

humanity comes from God. A second presupposition is that there is one constant, God. There simply was nothing before Him. The phrase, *the immutability of God,* is defined as "God cannot change in being, perfections, purpose, and promise."[8] This is the bedrock of how we see God. If He were able to change, we could have no security of tomorrow, let alone an eternity in the new heaven. Process theism is the belief that God is in process and nothing is fixed or known.[9] This teaching holds that God is finite. There is always the potential that God could die or go away. Everything in the future is unknown even to God. This teaching was proposed to allow for the maximum ability for people to make free choices. In creation, the Process Theist holds that God only set things up for us, and it is up to humanity to do the best that can be done. If this teaching were true, there could never be true salvation. What are we being saved from? God cannot be an eternal, holy God that is just and merciful. If our choices dictate His actions, then we could lose our salvation not only as we live on earth, but if God can change, then we might go to heaven when we die, only for Him to change His mind and place everyone in hell. His promises become meaningless, and there is no lasting hope. Observing more of these passages helps us see that the "always" before His attributes gives us security in who we are as a creation. His perfections and other attributes allow His people to know that even while we are damaged and sinful, He is always there with the same attributes He has always possessed.

A third presupposition is that the Bible is reliable in all that it teaches and gives authority to all doctrines that the church holds. As found in the Evangelical Dictionary of Theology, "History is the laboratory in which theology tests its ideas. We must conclude that the departure from belief in the complete trustworthiness of the Bible

---

8 Ibid, 163.
9 Walter Elwell, Evangelical Dictionary of Theology Vol 2. Baker Academic: Grand Rapids, 2002, page 1182

is a very serious step, not only in terms of what it does to this one doctrine but even more in terms of what happens to other doctrines as a result."[10] The doctrine of the Trinity is the nerve center and foundation of all our other doctrines. The mystery of the Trinity is so interwoven that one item will greatly affect all other doctrines. For example, if we looked at Deuteronomy 6 and see that we are to worship one God and then see that Jesus is saying he is "another" God, we are no longer monotheistic and one part of the Bible is wrong. This one error turns into a crack that leads to more issues. It will be discovered that the Father, Son, and Holy Spirit are all persons of the Trinity, but one in essence. If we lose this doctrine of the Bible, there will be major changes to all beliefs.

---

10 Erickson, 196.

CHAPTER 1
One in Essence

The defining characteristics of God make up His essence. It is the unchanging parts or characteristics that help humanity know who God is by studying the scriptures. The word defined by Unger states that "Essence (from the Lat. Verb *esse,* "to be") signifies that which a person or thing is in himself or itself, apart from all that is accidental. . . Theology has often made large use of these terms in its attempts to arrive at the proper and scriptural conception of God."[11] To be one in essence means certain characteristics set a standard for being. Here again, we will state the presupposition that the Bible is true and that there are no errors found in it. We will also presume that all the authority of the Bible was given to man in the Bible, and it is reliable in all of its teachings. Then, from this starting point, the examination of the characteristics of the essence of God will begin. God is the definition of love. He is the spirit. He is worthy of worship. He is the one who sets moral laws and is never within time, or space, or limited by power. By examining these characteristics, we will get a better definition of who God is, and then the investigation will turn to the persons of the Trinity and to how each of their characteristics fits both the essence of God and at the same time fulfills their part of their personage.

---

11 Merrill F Unger, The New Unger's Bible Dictionary (Chicago: Moody Press, 1988), 375.

When the phrase "God is…" is used, it gives Him character or a description so He can be known. There must be a bit of caution as to how the phrases are read and meant to be understood. If we say God is holy, then one can assume that when we look for God, we will find holiness. While this is true, we must be cautious with the word *is*. In the culture today, we can be correct in saying that Jerry is nice, but to equate Jerry and nice is not what *is* meant. While yes, most of the time Jerry participates in actions that are defined as nice, Jerry can be mean at times. Jerry being nice 95% of the time helps us define Jerry as nice. Now, when we return to the attributes of God, we are not saying God is mostly loving or almost perfect. The definitions mentioned here will equate the characterization of His attribute with its proper definition. When humanity loves, it is based on the character of God, not the action defining God. If someone shows love to a neighbor by bringing cookies, then the neighbor is using God's characteristic of love and concern. The person doing the action is simply trying to achieve the standard God has for His people, and that standard is God. The Bible helps us see this with a passage in Isaiah chapter 6. The heavenly beings are praising God and saying holy, holy, holy.[12] The phrase repeated three times is the superlative for the ultimate holy. The reader should be drawn to the fact that anything holy needs to be placed on the scale of who God is. If it does not meet the qualifications of God, then it is not holy in its purest form. One of the unchanging characteristics of God is that He is love. In English, the word love is defined in a variety of ways. The English word can mean a great fondness for something, a brotherly appreciation, a sexual feeling, or it can be described as an unconditional relationship built on unity, communication, and trust.[13] The English language has only this one word to fulfill all of these definitions. The Greek, however, has several

---

12 Is 6:8
13 David B. Guralnik, Websters: New World Dictionary of the American Language, (Cleveland: William Collins, 1980), 838.

words that are translated into the English word love. The first step is to determine what word is used in the passages concerning God. Scripture tells us that God *is* love.[14] ἀγάπη is the word used, and it is only used in reference to the love that only God possesses or gives to His people. One of the key passages Jesus used to distinguish the two different forms of love is John 21:15. This is one of the last conversations Jesus has with Peter before Christ leaves His earthly ministry. Here Jesus asks the question, "Peter, do you love me?" Peter responds to Jesus by using, φιλῶ, *philo,* translated I have brotherly affection (for you). But that is not what Jesus was asking. Jesus was asking the first two times, Do you ἀγαπᾶς, *agape* me? With this word, Jesus wants an unconditional, unifying, obedient relationship with all that Peter was, and he could not give it. The third time, Jesus changes His word to φιλῶ, having a brotherly affection. Peter becomes grieved when he realizes that it is all he can give.[15] The whole passage is often missed due to English word usage. It makes the definition come alive when we realize that, ἀγαπᾶς, love is what Jesus is requesting of Peter, but all he could give was human affection. Agape love can only be obtained with the power of God. To determine if the essence of the one being called God is true, He must be the definition of ἀγαπᾶς, love.

The next definition of God's essence is truth. "He is spirit, and those who worship Him must worship in spirit and truth."[16] The passage concerns Jesus telling the Samaritan woman that God the Father is commanding all of His creation to worship Him. He tells her it does not matter where you worship, but it does matter how you worship. God is not defined by a place, and Jesus has told her that the

---

14 1 Jn. 4:8(HCSB).
15Archibald T. Robertson, Word Pictures in the New Testament: Vol 4 The Fourth Gospel, The Epistle to the Hebrews, (Nashville: Broadman Press, 1960), 321.
16 Jn. 4:24 (HCSB).

time for worship has come, and He is sharing with everyone how this can happen. God is not in a fixed location where we have to go to a special place to be with Him. We do have to understand that He is Spirit, and to worship Him, you must come in Spirit and truth.[17] There will be no hiding anything from God during worship.

The truth of worship can only be found in the worship of God. Jesus claims this by saying, "I am the way, the truth, and the life. No one comes to the Father except through me." "If you know Me, you will also know My Father. From now on, you do know Him and have seen Him."[18] Every word from Jesus has this claim: all I say is true. Therefore, if Jesus has one characteristic or statement that is not true, He cannot be God. Jesus is claiming that in order to see the Father, all you have to do is look at His Son, who stands before them. He is letting His followers know that all the promises that were being made have the promise of both the Father and the Son, and to rest assured, all of His words will happen.[19] Jesus was always willing to let the disciples know that there would be an ending to His ministry on earth, but it was the undeniable truth of His words that would help them through.

The next characteristic or attribute of God is where He says, "I am."[20] There are even passages that tell us that "I Am" is His name.[21] This is God's way of saying that His being has always been. He is outside of time.[22] He will not have an end.[23] Man will never be able to fit God into a box. God's existence is further than can ever be reached or even fathomed. After just a quick look at the vastness of

---

17 Robertson, 66-67.
18 Jn. 14:6-7 (HCSB).
19 Robertson, 250.
20 Jn. 8:58
21 Jn. 8:58, Rev. 1:8, Ex. 3:14.
22 Jb. 36:26.
23 Ps. 90:2, Ex. 3:14.

God, it makes one realize just how small humanity really is, yet still, He wants to have a loving relationship with His creation. The transcendence and imminence of God help the Christian see that God not only has the ability to see all things above, but he is also in the smallest details. It has been documented that for over 4,000 years, man has tried to understand the universe through astronomy. Many believed that the Muslim astronomers were trying to know a transcendent god and were some of the earliest observers of the stars. [24] As of 2022 A.D., we can almost calculate that there are more than 10 billion galaxies in the universe. Many believe that with the new telescope, we will probably find at least twice that many.[25] Christians, too, looked to the outer universe for a better understanding of the Creator, but Christians also understands that God is with us in the smallest details of our lives as well. The Creator of the vast universe has chosen a people on one planet with billions of options and came to us for a relationship. Whatever you ask in My name, I will do it so that the Father may be glorified in the Son."[26] The omnipotence of God shows us that He is able to do all that is within all of His holy will.[27] He has created all and is the ruler of all. Being the creator of all leads the scholar to the understanding that God is also omnipresent. There is nowhere He is not. Deuteronomy 10:14, Jeremiah 23:23-24, and Psalm 139:7-10 are a few examples of His Spirit being everywhere. This makes it possible to worship Him in any location, and it also keeps us from hiding anything from His knowledge. It is a short, logical leap to see that if God is everywhere and we cannot hide anything from Him, He would also know all things. This makes Him omniscient.[28] It is with great humility that we see God move in the

---

24 https://www.britannica.com/science/astronomy/History-of-astronomy
25 https://universemagazine.com/en/james-webb-helps-clarify-the-number-of-galaxies-in-the-universe/
26 Jn. 14:13 (HCSB).
27 Lk. 1:37, Mt. 19:26.
28 Jb. 37:16, Heb. 4:13, Mt. 10:29-30.

smallest parts of our lives. God has the ability to not only hold the universe in His control, but He is also in the tiniest parts of our being. Just as the astronomer looks to the galaxies, doctors are now looking at how we were created to determine how God works in the smallest parts of our bodies. In the latest research, physicians have been able to work on using our own immunity to combat cancer and other viruses. There are several breakthroughs both coming and that have been made that rely on the new knowledge of just how intricate God has made humanity.[29] The "I Am" of God and his nature has all looking to Him, even if people will not acknowledge His role in the sustaining nature of a transcendent and imminent God.

The essence of God is not only discovered in His personality and general attributes alone. There is another set of attributes that must be discussed, His moral attributes. If God is omniscient, omnipresent, and omnipotent, then His very nature dictates what is moral and right. The Scriptures tell us that God is holy.[30] Isaiah 6:3 tells of the angels in the act of worship to the holy, holy, holy God. This is the Hebrew way of saying that He is the very definition of holy, set aside as perfection.[31] Anything less than God loses out to His holiness. Because He asks us to be like Him, it is fair to say that He will never tempt another to be less.[32] Due to His character of being holy and true, it is easy to see that He is jealous to protect His honor.[33]

---

29 https://www.cancer.org/treatment/treatments-and-side-effects/treatment-types/immunotherapy/cancer-vaccines.html
30 Is. 6:3, Mt. 6:9.
31 Geoffery W.Grogan, The Expositor's Bible Commentary: Isaiah, Jeremiah, Lamentations, Ezekiel. ed.by Frank E. Gaebelein (Grand Rapids: Zondervan, 1986), 55.
32 Jms. 1:13.
33 1 Co. 4:7.

To best define the nature of God, we will look at the passages that give a direct description of Himself to His people. God is one, and His people are to be monotheistic. The clearest passage about the oneness of God starts with a declaration or announcement. "Listen, Israel: The Lord is our God, the Lord is One."[34] The word, שְׁמַע, *shema,* "should be seen as a word with great emphasis. The word is translated Hear! or Listen! It is a word that would create an image of someone yelling to a crowd, 'A tornado warning is being issued, take cover!'"[35] This is Moses telling the people, you must stop all that you are doing because the next thing I say will be of utmost importance. The Lord is to be our God, and He alone should be worshiped. יְהוָה is the Hebrew for the proper name for God, Yahweh. As a singular God to be worshiped in all areas of life, the people around would not automatically understand. These surrounding people groups were from a polytheistic worldview. This had been in place for all the surrounding people groups, including Egypt and the new land of Israel. To ensure that Israel understood what He was saying, He inserted the oneness of His essence through the giving of His name, Yahweh.[36] No other gods, local or universal, should be considered.

It is natural that people have wanted to place their personal feelings on who God is and who He is not. All people want is a just God and will fight for justice to prevail. However, not all have the same conclusion as to the understanding of the outcome. Without exception, we have our own blinders on when it comes to our thinking as to a just outcome. To the family who had someone murdered, the family believes justice is the killing of the murderer. To the family of the murderer, justice is true rehabilitation and possibly time served to

---

34 Dt. 6:4 (HCSB).
35 Dt. 6:4 (HCSB).
36 James Wolfendale, The Preacher's Complete Homiletic Commentary on the Fifth Book of Moses Called Deuteronomy, (Grand Rapids: Baker Books, 1996), 132-133.

get right with society. Which is justice? When it comes to all sin, God tells us that all are sinners and "fall short of the glory of God."[37] That being said, all deserve hell, and none can claim a right to enter heaven. It is understandable that we want justice in the world of sin. What if a person never has the chance to hear, or what if the truth were never told? Is it just to condemn the person to hell? C. S. Lewis was one of Christianity's greatest minds, but in the book, *The Last Battle,* Lewis tells the reader that the character who wholeheartedly worshiped a false God would get credit for that worship from the true God. Even when the character mentioned that he hated Aslan, the Christ character, and followed His enemy.[38] It does not hold with scripture that someone who worshiped a false God, even if he worked to do the will of the true God at one time, like Balaam in the book of Numbers, can receive forgiveness for worshiping another God. Balaam was judged by God and was killed in an Israelite raid that was a judgement on Balaam's people in Joshua 13:22. 2 Peter 2:10-15 makes it clear that even a man used by God, such as Balaam, has no excuse for his wickedness and was justly punished. Lewis' belief in credited righteousness does not hold true. It is not for us to hope for the salvation of those who have not heard. It is our duty, according to Matthew 28:19, to go and tell them. God is just, and Christians need to understand that we live in a fallen world full of injustice. It is the Christian's responsibility to trust that when all is said and done, God will be fully just.

The oneness of God does not stop when the Israelites enter their new land. It is clear that there is to be an ongoing emphasis on the oneness of God. It is to be a priority for the chosen people.[39] They were being told that no other God exists, and they are to serve with

---

37 Romans 3:23
38 C. S. Lewis, The Last Battle, Macmillan Company: New York: 1970. p. 165
39 Dt. 4:35-39; 32:39

this declaration. Later, when the people beg God for a king in 1 Samuel and God decides that the people will have a monarchy, He makes it clear that even a king is not to be placed above Him. He is still the single essence to be worshiped.[40] The admonition to ensure that God is one has been taught and accepted throughout all of the Old Testament from Genesis to Zechariah. On that day, Yahweh will become King over all the earth—Yahweh alone, and His name alone.[41]

The New Testament is also in agreement concerning the oneness of God. Jesus emphasized this by saying, "Listen, Israel! The Lord our God, the Lord is One. Love the Lord your God with all your heart, with all your soul, with all your mind, and with all your strength."[42] This is Jesus telling His followers that the oneness of God today is the same as it was yesterday. Not only is this the greatest command, but it is also connected to salvation.[43] Monotheism is repeated in the Greek, *ego emi*, or the "I am" passages, stating that Jesus is the one God. This can be noted in Acts 17:22 and 1 Corinthians 8.[44]

Salvation does start with the understanding that God is one, and it is through this one God that salvation must come. It also must be understood that just knowing the information is not enough. "You believe that God is one; you do well. The demons also believe—and they shudder."[45] Even God's enemies understand that He is one in essence. They have already been punished and will not be saved, so there will not be salvation for those who just intellectually know that God is one.

---

40 2 Sm. 7:22, 1 Kg. 8:60, 2 Kg. 5:15, and 1 Ch. 17:20.
41 Zch. 14:9.
42 Mk. 12:29 (HCSB).
43 Jn. 17:3. Rm. 3:30.
44 Sproul, 9:00 min.
45 Jms. 2:19.

In college and seminary, the professors go over the different levels, or stages, of learning. Nothing merely appears to us, and we are able to do it for the first time. The closest example would be a talented musician who can seemingly pick up any instrument and begin playing within an hour. While they can pick something up quickly and the tune might come soon, the stages of learning are the same. What makes the instrument work? Is it air by reed, air by buzzing, or is it percussion? Then how do the notes change? What is the range of notes? All these questions must be addressed before any tune can come out. In the same way, it takes time to better understand what God wants for our lives. There is a great desire to just get the information and start using it. The first step is just reading the passages. Then you might start memorizing the words. This is an important part of what we do to learn about God and His instructions. Psalm 119:11 tells us to hide the word of God in our hearts. This implies that we take the next steps. In the hierarchy of learning, memorizing is the lowest step. The steps, according to LeRoy Ford, are: knowledge, comprehension, application, analysis, synthesis, and evaluation.[46] We begin by memorizing, but by the end of our study, the student will be able to take the verse and apply it directly and indirectly, as well as evaluate the overall meaning in life concerning not just a simple passage, but see how the passage of a characteristic of God should be applied to many areas of the student's life. Just as the musician starts with a single note and can move to playing with a full symphony over time, our study of the Trinity will eventually touch every other area of our spiritual life and quite possibly the lives of many others.

––––––––––––––––––

46 LeRoy Ford, Design for Teaching and Training: A Self-Study Guide to Lesson Planning, Nashville: Broadman Press, 1978. P. 101.

God has given people some of His attributes that set Him apart from all else. When God said that He was love, He is stating that the very definition of love is wrapped in His personal character. He cannot be anything less than love. While using just ten of God's characteristics, we discover a lot about the essence of God. Later, it will be discovered how the Persons of the Trinity will be mysteriously understood to have all these unique qualities.

Looking at the essence of God is a great way to start a study of the Trinity, but there also needs to be a time of self-reflection. How one sees God is important, but how does the church live up to His character? The funeral home is one place in our society where most stop and reflect. What was a friend known for or stood for? Even better, if that were me in the casket, what would others say about me and my character? Take the time to ask a close friend what they see in you the most. Ask them to write out the characteristics that best describe your essence. Have them be as honest as possible. While the other is looking over their list, make a list of all the character traits that you see as the most important. Now it is understood that no one will live up to Christ, but a person with the name Christian should do their all to live up to their new name. When a person accepts Christ as their Lord and Savior, He changes their name to be a child of God. As children of God, it is our responsibility to live up to His essence, not our old name. With a great passion and a great helper in the Holy Spirit, strive for the essence of God.

CHAPTER 2
The Father as God

I t is now established that God is one in essence, and many of His characteristics have been identified. These few characteristics cannot fully detail who God is; however, it must be determined if each of the persons of the Trinity fits with His one essence. The irony here is that when looking at the Bible, one finds the Father, the Son, and the Holy Spirit. They all claim to be God, and they claim that the other two are also God without violating monotheism. How can this be understood? In this brief section, a careful textual examination of the already mentioned essence of God passages will be tested against the claims of the Father, then the Son, and then the Holy Spirit. As it will be shown, they all possess the single essence of God. A study on how this mystery can be explained will come later in the book.

The Father possesses the unique qualities of God and is in full possession of God's essence. First, the Father is said to be the definer of love. In Hebrews, it is seen that discipline is a definitive way to know if there is love between a parent and a child. Hence, a lack of discipline is a sign of a lack of love. His children will know of His love by understanding that He shows His love for His adopted children. If a person is living in contradiction to the Father and the individual is not being disciplined, then the individual is not His child because His love has not been given.[47] The Father's love of His people will be evident to all.

The Father is spirit and desires that His creation worship Him in spirit. The people must also worship Him in truth. John 4:23-24 is very clear and pointed when it says, God is Truth. It is here that Jesus, the Son, is showing the woman at the well that God the Father is spirit, and He is to be worshiped in spirit and in truth. God's creation is only to worship Him and Him alone.[48] In John 4, Jesus is telling the woman that there will be a time of worship to the Father. Therefore, Jesus, knowing the Exodus scriptures, is telling the woman that the Father is God, and he alone is to be worshiped.

There are four words that are used for the single English word *worship*. There are Hebrew words, and one is a Greek word used for our one English word. In this case, almost all of them have the same definition: humble submission to a man or deity whereby the person gives due reverence with a physical act of respect and adoration.[49] The act of worship that the Father desires is very specific. He first states that He alone is worthy of worship. He is a jealous God, and no other is to be worshiped.[50] There are times when angelic beings show up, and people are overwhelmed by their brilliance. In Revelation 19:10, John bows, and the messenger quickly rebuffs and directs worship back to God. The proper acts of worship to the Father are described throughout Numbers and Leviticus. This is the way you are to worship. With the act of worship, the Father dictates that obedience comes first. There are times when the Father is not worshiped, and

---

47 Heb. 12:6-9.
48 Ex. 20:4-5.
49 Merril F. Unger, The New Unger's bible Dictionary. R.K. Harrison editor. Moody Press: Chicago, 1988, p. 1373.
50 Exodus 34:13; Deuteronomy 6:13; Lukc 4:8

God and the people need to be reminded that worship is only for God. Habakkuk 2:18-20 said it best,

"What prophet is the idol when its maker has carved it, or an image, a teacher of falsehood? For its maker trusts in his own handiwork when he fashions speechless idols. Woe to him who says to a piece of wood, 'Arise!' And that is your teacher? Behold, it is overlaid with gold and silver, and there is no breath at all inside it. But the Lord is in His holy temple. Let all the earth be silent before Him."

People will place their own accomplishments above God and thus make their own creation a God. People must repent of all sin and become holy. In Hebrews 10:1-13, it states that worship and holiness go hand in hand, and worship in the New Testament comes to the Father through the Son. The act of worship is still directed to the Father, and the relationship of the Father to His created children is very important and must be further explored.

The Old Testament shows that the Father has great patience with His people, but His patience only goes so far. In Malachi 2:10, the passage states that the Lord desires a relationship with His children. That relationship is secure as the Creator and Father of mankind. However, the worship of the people to God is affected by how we interact with other people. An act of sin against another person not only affects the person-to-person relationship, but it also affects our relationship with God. Parents can tell you that if Johnny hits his sister with a ball on purpose, the sister is not the only one who gets angry at Johnny. The parent who watches the event will have something to say about the aggressive action. The same is true with God. Now, if Johnny wants to be in good graces with his parents again, he will need to truly apologize to his sister. He may need to apologize for breaking the family rules as well, and he will need to change his future actions. It would be hard to imagine that his continued hitting of his sister would be found favorable to the sister or the parent. It would be even harder to imagine that he could get away with hitting his sister by bringing his parents gifts of flowers from the yard. It seems to be bordering on the absurd, but Malachi 2:13 states that the people were worshiping with full emotional giving and sacrifice, but God rejected the worship. People cannot see the Father because He is Spirit. The problem is God does see us, and as the Father, He has something to say. The Christian may not notice that God has seen, but every act is known by the Father.

To worship God the Father, one must be purified of all sin.[51] This purification process is serious, takes commitment, and in some cases, it is painful. The Old Testament passage of Isaiah 6 mentions an angelic being coming to him with a live coal to purify his lips. The holiness of God is always overwhelming. In the New Testament, 1 Corinthians 5:1-5, Paul tells the church that there is a time to hand a church member over to Satan. He finishes the chapter by telling the church that they are to judge the insider. Those outside the church are known to be full of sin and in need of great repentance. The worthiness to worship also appears throughout all of 1 Corinthians, but especially in 1 Corinthians 11:27-32. When it comes to worship through the Lord's Supper, a Christian is to self-examine himself so he is not guilty of the blood and body of the Son. Worship to the Father must be conducted within a correct relationship with the Father.

When people find themselves in sin, God is faithful and loving in letting people return to worship and restore the proper relationship. This only comes from true repentance, and a price has to be paid for sin. It is not good enough to be sorry. People in a proper relationship with God the Father must be holy. The whole sacrificial system of the Old Testament was based on the seriousness of sin. Romans 3:23 tells us, "all have sinned and fall short of the glory of God." The Father

---

51 Mal 3:3, Is 6:7

15

made this possible by sending the Son to the world to live a perfect life and to die as a perfect sacrifice so we might be in good standing with Him. The death of the Son shows just how important God takes our relationship with His creation. The restoration is not always quick and easy. When people sin, they turn to selfish ambition. It is good to know that God is slow to judge and is great in mercy; however, if the Christian continues in sin, he will be disciplined.

The end of Hebrews 10, starting in verse 32, says that life may not be easy for the Christian, but Christians must stay the course and remain close to God. There are times when confrontation concerning sin is needed. Going back to 1 Corinthians 5, a man in the church has committed a moral and public outrage. He has been confronted with his sin by the people of the church on a personal level, and he has not repented. Then the news reached Paul. Paul tells the church that if the man does not repent, remove him from the church and treat him as a non-Christian. The hope through the process is not to be the punisher of sin, but to restore this man to Christ.

The Western church is so concerned with being sued or being labeled as unloving or bigoted that there is very limited adherence to the discipline the Father asks. It might also be that the church is so far removed from this practice that the people do not know where to start. As a result, the church has lost repentance on the whole. This makes the church no different than the rest of the world. The logic follows that the western church has also lost its ability to worship God the Father as dictated. The church will be judged, or the church will repent. Worship of the Holy Father is a necessity for a relationship to thrive. Rest assured, He will discipline those He loves. The ability of the Father to know our thoughts and actions comes from the attributes that show how he functions in space and time.

The Father is omnipresent, meaning He is in all places at all times. No matter where we are, we cannot hide from the Father. He knows our every action. When we pray, we are to do it in secret because the Father hears us in all the places we think we can hide, and He is to get all the glory.[52] In Luke 12:30, Jesus has assured the people that the Father truly knows all of their needs. He also knows everything about everyone because of His omnipresence. The other attribute of absoluteness is seen in His power. For this trait, we apply the term omnipotence. He designed and created everything in the beginning, and we have the Father demonstrating His power by raising the dead.[53] He even states that He will do even more wonderful things to show His power.[54] The Father's power is also in the immutability of God. He does not change and will always be there to understand His people. When we pray, we are to pray to the holy and honored Father.[55] He is the supplier of all we need and the ruler of all things.

The proper name of the Father, Yahweh, reveals to Moses that there is one thing everyone needs to know about him. He is the great "I Am." This most simplistic saying demonstrates that God was before you and God will be here after you die. There is nothing more to say about God. The Father will never change, and we can be assured that the Father is God and He is one.[56]

---

52 M.t 6:6, Ps. 139.
53 Jn. 11:21-27.
54 Jn. 5:21.
55 Mt. 6:9.
56 Ex. 3:14.

CHAPTER 3
The Son as God

It would be completely understandable to complete our search for God with the Father, but in this section, it will be discovered that another Person of the Godhead is claiming the same essence as the Father. The Son of God, Jesus Christ, is the second person of the Trinity. Part of knowing Jesus as God comes from understanding His name. As said by Sinclair Ferguson and Alistair Begg, "Jesus Christ has been given the name above all names. The names assigned to him begin in Genesis and end in Revelation. Taken together, they express the incomparable character of Jesus Christ our Savior and Lord."[57] The word *Lord* here is the same action of humble submission stated under the Father. This is a direct indication that people are to worship the Son. Passages like Romans 10:9-10 indicate that "Jesus" and "Lord" must go together to be fully understood. Paul makes it clear that a person must confess Jesus as Lord of their life to be saved. Another passage that deals with the eternal characteristics of Jesus is "In the beginning was the Word (logos), and the Word was with God and the Word was God."[58] It is clear that John was equating the word (*logos*) here with Jesus. This goes way beyond Jesus being a great man who was chosen by God to live a good enough life and could be the sacrifice needed for sin. God set the sacrificial system up in the beginning to require a perfect sacrifice; the animal was to be one

---

57 Alistair Begg and Sinclair Ferguson. Name Above all Names. (Wheaton, Crossway, 2013), 15.
58 Jn. 1:1 (HCSB).

without blemish.[59] The second the person sinned again, there was a need for another sacrifice. To end the cycle, God would need to implement a special sacrifice. From the fall of Adam in Genesis 3, no person is capable of living outside sin. Even if someone could live a perfect life, it would not be enough to appease the wrath and judgement of man just on that criterion. The ultimate sacrifice must be brought by God.

This passage also tells the reader that Jesus was before the beginning of time. He never came into being. He always was and always will be. He was the Word that brought all things into existence at creation. Jesus goes beyond being just a man; He was God and always has been God. The discussion of His role in the Trinity will be explored later. John 1:29 shows that Jesus has come to take away the sins of the world. As we have seen before, the only one who can make something holy is God. Jesus was a part of the redemption plan of man before man came into being. He was willing to become a human and then lay down his human life because He loved His people, and He knew that only God could provide a sufficient, perfect, and holy offering. He told his disciples, "Greater love has no one than this, that one lay down his life for his friends."[60] Jesus in Romans 5:8 proves that He went way above the love one man can give his brother. If the greatest love a man can give is his life for a friend, then He went above that love to die for those who were His enemies, full of sin. When we look at sacrificial living or a vocation requiring sacrifice, we often look to the military. This occupation, over all others, makes one understand the need to be close as a group and helps the serviceman understand that the lives of those in the platoon are a single unit fighting as one. A comrade in arms who is willing to go to the point of death for his friends in war is willing to make the ultimate sacrifice.

---

59 Lev. 22:17-23
60 Jn. 15:13 (NASB).

That is why the Medal of Honor, which has been awarded to a few men and one woman to date, is often awarded to the individuals posthumously. This medal is the United States' highest military honor. To receive this honor, "the deed performed must have been one of personal bravery or self-sacrifice so conspicuous as to clearly distinguish the individual above his comrades and must have involved risk of life."[61] This great act of heroism is the best a person can do. However, here we see that the Son not only left heaven to come to live with us on earth, but He then showed us the greatest example of living with no sin. This alone still did not meet the requirement of the Father to fix all of man's sin issues. The Son "laid down His life for the ransom of many."[62] He died, and after three days, He rose again for the unrepentant sinner who opposes His will. He was willing to be obedient to His Father and present a holy sacrifice for the sins of the people. Jesus died so whosoever will may have eternal life.[63] It goes above what any man could do. His sacrifice is something only a perfect God could provide.

The attributes of omnipresence, omnipotence, and omniscience are harder to see in the Son's earthly ministry, but the Son is beyond His earthly ministry. When Jesus came as a man, He did not just come into being. He was not created but begotten. This will be addressed later, but as stated above, He created all things and sustains the entire universe from the beginning of what we know of as time.[64] This part may be somewhat hard to comprehend, but Jesus did know the hearts of men. When it was time for Jesus to choose His disciples, He knew what Nathanael was doing before they even met. Jesus surprised him

---

61Laura Jowdy, C.A., Archivist & Collections Manager, Congressional Medal of Honor Society. Medal of Honor a Primer,
https://www.cmohs.org/media/24881.pdf/view. May 2019. (Accessed December 12, 2022.)
62 Matthew 20:28
63 Jn. 3:16.
64 Jn. 1, Heb. 1:1-6.

by telling him that he was standing under a tree before being called. Jesus knew his name before being introduced. Nathanael's reaction was to worship Jesus. Jesus did not stop him because He is worthy of worship. Worship was for God alone, and Jesus did not refuse it. He built on it, saying, "You will see greater things than this."[65]

Jesus clearly declares, "'I am' the way, the truth, and the life."[66] John 8:58 takes it up several levels by emphatically saying, "I Am." This name was reserved for the God of Abraham. To meet the qualifications of the essence of God, the Son would have to manifest this attribute. The reaction was such that the religious leaders fully believed Jesus was claiming to be the same as God. The religious leaders took up stones at once to kill Him. They would only react like this if someone had just declared themselves to be equal to God. This is exactly what Jesus was doing. He was saying that He and the Father are one in essence.[67] These passages state that Jesus was claiming his unchanging character as God.

Jesus was wholly man and wholly God. This is how we can explain the time Jesus went to his disciples after the resurrection and before the ascension and ate food with them. Jesus had them place their hands into his wounds. These acts speak to His humanity, but they also state that the disciples were gathered together in a room behind locked doors, and Jesus entered the room without the need of a door or a key. This was Jesus as Spirit doing as He wished. The Son wanted to be with His friends.[68] After His ascension to heaven, He is seen in the story of the stoning of Stephen. The Son was in His proper place, standing next to the Father in heaven. Jesus is the rightful ruler on His heavenly throne. Only God can have such a position. This is

---

65 Jn. 1:50.
66 Jn. 14:6.
67 Jn. 10:30.
68 Jn. 20:19-26.

one of the few occurrences where two persons of the Trinity are together and distinguished. The distinguishing characteristics of the Son will be dealt with in a future chapter. The most compelling verse is Acts 7:59, which says, "they went on stoning Stephen as he called on the Lord and said, 'Lord Jesus, receive my Spirit!'" Stephen and those recording this story openly acknowledged that they serve the monotheistic God of Abraham. At the same time, they declare worship for the Son, Jesus Christ. Even with both having the essence of deity, Stephen asked the Son to receive his spirit as he was in the process of dying. Clearly, the all-powerful Son will take care of our spirits as we enter heaven.[69] There can be little doubt that the Son has continued His eternal function of God even after His ascension, and people are to worship Him with reverence.

---

69 Acts 7:54-60

CHAPTER 4
The Holy Spirit as God

When considering the singular essence of God, it seems to be quite a stretch to think of the Father and the Son as having the same essence. Now we must reconcile a third claimant to the oneness of God. The Holy Spirit is the Third person of the Trinity who makes a claim to the same character of the singular essence. The Holy Spirit has two of His attributes designated within His name. He is holy and worthy to be worshiped, and that worship is possible through the power of the Spirit in Christ.[70] It should be noted that the Spirit will always connect worship with the Son. He is the Spirit of God, and without the Holy Spirit, a person has no hope for salvation.[71] All three are in agreement that there is one God, and all three acknowledge each other in their roles as distinguished persons. Even though He reflects the worship of the Son, He has a special place in the salvation and worship of the believer. One example is that people are to worship God in spirit.[72] This requires a person who engages in worship to be in sync with the Holy Spirit for true worship to even be possible. This mandates that the Holy Spirit is acting in God's essence.

---

70 Heb. 9:14.
71 Rm. 8:9.
72 Jn. 4:24

The Spirit demonstrates the three omnis of the one essence: omnipresence, omniscience, and omnipotence. These are the same attributes ascribed to the Father and to the Son in previous chapters. Starting with omnipresence, it must be understood that God is both transcendent and immanent in nature. Genesis 1 begins with the Spirit hovering over the newly created universe. This action is more than just hovering over and observing an object. It is demonstrating that God is over the whole universe in its every detail.[73] He is ensuring that the work is to the perfect specifications of the Father. In every detail, the Spirit is actively preparing the exact specifications of the Architect. This can only be possible if the Spirit is everywhere and working with the other persons of the Trinity. Even with the Holy Spirit being over the creation, the Spirit of God in Psalm 139 demonstrates that God is both all-knowing and all-present. Saying, "Where can I go from your Spirit? or where can I flee from your presence?"[74] Even when being formed in our mother's womb, God's Spirit is there with a plan for the making of all of life.[75] These are just two examples of the Spirit of God being used in the pre-birth ordering of a man's life in the Old Testament. The Spirit is actively involved even in the mother's womb. There is no place the Spirit of God does not reside. The New Testament is even clearer about the Holy Spirit's involvement in the most intimate areas of a person's life. The first is when Jesus was conceived by the Holy Spirit.[76] Even before Joseph knew that his bride-to-be was with child, the Holy Spirit had impregnated Mary. She would be the mother of the Son of God. This is the one and only time the Holy Spirit creates a new life post-initial creation. This demonstrated just how powerful and all-understanding the Holy Spirit is in the world. The Son of God had to have the Spirit

---

73 Gn 1:2
74 Ps. 139:7-8 (HCSB).
75 Jer. 1:4-5, Lk 1:35
76 Mt 1:18

to begin the salvific plan for mankind. The Spirit's activity in the Son's childhood story does not end there. When Mary entered a room while pregnant with Jesus, Elizabeth was filled with the Holy Spirit, and her unborn baby, John, acknowledges the Son of God inside Mary by leaping inside her.[77] Looking back to Jesus' teaching on whom God demonstrates the power He has and shows that God is Spirit, and those who worship Him must worship in Spirit and truth.[78] The Spirit's activity does not stop there. The Holy Spirit, later, was sent to indwell each person who accepts the Son as Savior and Lord.[79] There is no doubt that the Spirit is in every location.

It is also evident in many of these same passages that He is all powerful. How else could He control the universe without help? How could He call a prophet? His eternal nature is found from the first chapter of Genesis to the last chapter in Revelation. He was going all over the earth at creation and was a part of all creation.[80] It was the Spirit that was present for Jesus' entire ministry, and He was the one who was there to raise Him from the dead.[81] Just to add to His claim to power, He is also with the Christian in all places, and at the same time, He is able to help us through anything. Romans 8:14 shows that "For all who are led by the Spirit of God are sons of God."

The scripture points out that the role of the Spirit is one full of power and is extremely important. The scripture even warns the reader to take seriously the relationship between the Spirit and the people. Matthew 12:30-31 states, "Anyone who is not with Me is against Me, and anyone who does not gather with Me scatters. Because of this, I tell you, people will be forgiven every sin and blasphemy, but the

---

77 Luke 1:39-45
78 Jn 4:24
79 1 Cor. 6:19-20
80 Gn. 1:2.
81 Rm. 8.8-11.

blasphemy against the Spirit will not be forgiven."[82] A person in the Old or New Testament had to be very serious with their speech and actions in regard to God. The religious rulers would even go as far as banning the proper name of God lest they stumble and use it incorrectly. Any high-handed, unacceptable usage of God's name was a death sentence.[83] Therefore, if Jesus, who claims to be God, said that the misuse of the Holy Spirit's name cannot be forgiven either here or in heaven, then He must possess the essence of the one true God. It is through the Spirit that a person understands what the Son has done for them. By rejecting the Spirit, you have rejected salvation and thereby rejected all of God.

The beginning of the church was full of great excitement. The church was growing very quickly, and the people were sharing all that they had with other believers. This is soon after Acts 1:8, where the Spirit's great power was poured out over the church. With the Spirit's power, the people spoke in the language of the hearer. The church was baptizing and growing quickly. All seemed to be going according to plan until the scriptures describe a couple that lied about their giving. By Acts 5, Ananias and Sapphira were brought to the church's attention. They had sold a piece of property and had given some of it to the church. The problem is that they said they gave the whole amount to the church when they had not. Peter was directed by the Holy Spirit that it was due to their lying to the Spirit that their life was now forfeit, and they fell dead. No one should take the Holy Spirit as a weaker or lesser person in the Trinity. The good news is that it is the Spirit that is loving in our weakness and is there for His people in everyday life. Romans 8:26 says, "Likewise, the Spirit helps us in our weakness. For we do not know what to pray for as we ought, but the

---

82 Mt. 12:30-31 (HCSB).
83Unger, 174.

Spirit himself intercedes for us with groanings too deep for words."[84] It goes on to say that no matter where the Christian finds themselves, the Spirit is there, full of power, and is willing to help. The Holy Spirit has all the characteristics of the one essence of God.

---

84 Rm 8:26

CHAPTER 5
The Mystery of the Trinity

The single essence of God is found in the three distinct persons: Father, Son, and Holy Spirit. There seems to be a logical fallacy in saying there are three persons, yet the Christian is monotheistic. This leads us to consider three options of logic. First, the statement is a contradiction and cannot be explained. This would end the debate as to having a defendable position. The second is a paradox. A paradox is where there seem to be two opposing positions, but logically they both work, and as a result, they can work together.[85] This, on the surface, seems to be the logic to follow, but when the word definitions are discovered, it is not found to be a paradox. The third is the mystery of the Trinity. A mystery is where one person understands the full meaning, but the other person finds it too difficult to explain.[86] God, in His full knowledge of Himself and the universe, is going to have a better understanding than man will have concerning how He works as God. As stated earlier, the concept of the Trinity is not a contradiction or a paradox, but it will be seen as a mystery.

The controversy of the mystery has only been greatly debated over the last 150 years. It will be noted in the next chapter that orthodox Christianity has been defending monotheism as having its roots from the beginning of time. Starting in Genesis, we learn that in the beginning, God made everything. The word "God" in these passages

---

85 Webster, "Paradox"
86 Webster, "Mystery"

is singular. Yet in these same passages, it has been noted that the Father, Son, and Holy Spirit were all active in creation, and the passages also support each person having the single essence of God. All three persons claim deity. The plural form of God can be seen in the Genesis 1:27 passage, "They (plural) created them male and female." This is the Elohim plural usage. It ends with a singular verb form. This is not a direct reference to the Trinity, but it is the first hint that God is showing more information about Himself.[87] Now, this looks like a contradiction with both a plural Godhead and a singular God. This would be a contradiction if it was said that God was three in essence and one in essence. It would also be a contradiction to say that God was three in person and one in person. However, the Bible teaches, and church historians have taught that He is one in essence and three in person.[88] Norman Geisler, in his *Systematic Theology,* sees no contradiction in having the three persons in one essence.

This is demonstrated by pointing out that the law of non-contradictions mandates that for two propositions to be contradictory, they must both affirm and deny something of (1) the same thing; (2) at the same time; and (3) in the same sense (in the same relationship). Clearly, this is not the case in affirming that God is one and only one in relation to His essence; God is more than one (viz., three) in relation to His persons. These are two different senses or relations. Therefore, the Trinity is not contradictory.[89]

Logically, He is not breaking the law of non-contradiction. This still leaves us with deciding just how this can be possible. One argument that supports the manifestations of God is progressive revelation. It is just the beginning of the possible explanations to see

---

87 Sproll, 14 min.
88 Ibid, 2 min
89 Norman Geisler, Systematic Theology. Vol. 2. (Minneapolis: Bethany House, 2003), 292-293.

how man, over time and generations, has come closer to understanding the concept of the Trinity. Progressive revelation means that as time passes, God gives more and more information to people. He never corrects His previous revelation, but rather builds on what He has already revealed. This is not to be confused with the modern progressive theology, where God does not know what tomorrow holds until it comes.[90]

The Father, Son, and Holy Spirit are here and active throughout all time. However, the Old Testament follower would not have known of the Son who would come to earth. He was simply not known to him. This does not mean that the Son came only after His incarnation. His work can be seen by those who are in the New Testament throughout all time. The Spirit would be the same Spirit of God in both the Old and New Testaments, but those who had the Spirit poured out on them at Pentecost have a fuller understanding because He was the one giving great power to a whole people group for the first time. Obviously, it tells us that it was the Holy Spirit who was the one who impregnated Mary at Jesus' annunciation. This has to be before the Son sent the Spirit to the people. These lessons are just the beginning of understanding this mystery.

A mystery is when one entity knows all the information, while another does not know and may never fully grasp or comprehend all the information. People were made finite and God, as we have discovered, is infinite: all-knowing, omniscient. The information God gives finite man is what man can handle in understanding who God is. It is much like a physics professor asking his class to solve an equation regarding the twin theory of relativity. This can be done; however, the class the professor is teaching is first-grade math, where they just learned two plus two is four. Now we can see that although

---

90Sproll, 3:40.

the information is possible, it is not accessible to be solved by this class. Even if a man cannot fully know God, it does not mean it is impossible for the information to be known. Wayne Grudem sums up this thought by saying the three persons are our way of saying something that remains a great mystery. "It is an existence far different from anything we have experienced." However, there is no contradiction.[91] The creation must accept what He has given us and follow His direction. In Paul House's book *Bonhoeffer's Seminary Vision*, House offers the reader the basic reason why we must worship God as He has revealed Himself.

"How Christians think about God determines how they think about everything else. After all, Christians believe God-Father, Son, and Holy Spirit are the Creator, Provider, and Redeemer of persons and history. He is Lord over all realms of life. His Word defines and directs what is good and right in every person, home, church, and ministry. A proper grasp of and adherence to theology is therefore essential for anyone or organization desiring reality and God-defined relevance."[92] This being the case, our search for the mystery of the Trinity needs to start with a basic understanding of three words. Unity indicates that there is only one God and not two or more. Simplicity means that there are not two or more parts in God. Tri-unity means there are three persons in one God.[93] If each decision we make is dependent on knowing God, then it makes it all the more important to dig deep into knowing all about Him. We must hear and discern His voice in our lives. His directions provide a trustworthy council and can be depended on for a firm foundation. Knowing God and His work will help the church with all of our moral obligations. Not doing this can cause the church to better understand His love through discipline.

---

91 Grudem, 255-256.
92Paul R. House, Bonhoeffer's Seminary Vision (Wheaton: Crossway, 2015), 1.
93 Geisler, 269.

He will love His people. It would be better all-around if we find that love in grace and mercy over discipline.

As we prepare to study the church fathers and how God has directed them to lead the church, we need to see that the basic understanding of the Trinity is being followed in all of its logical steps. Man is known to falter, and we must always be vigilant in our defense of the faith. God has always wanted His people to know him; however, from the time the Spirit was poured out on all Christians until today, God has been dealing with people on a direct basis. This is to coincide with church leaders working together to ensure that our relationship with God is kept in its proper form and meaning.

CHAPTER 6
Historical Background

The investigation into the Trinity's historical background begins with the word, Trinity. The word, Trinity, does not appear as a word in Hebrew, Greek, or Aramaic. There simply is not an occurrence in the Bible where this doctrine is neatly presented to the followers of the new church or any other section of Scripture. Having no references that use the word "Trinity" or even a description of the term we now use, it is difficult to express the meaning of the term that describes God and His nature and function. To best determine a theology from this point of view, there must be a thorough search of the Scripture for indicators and clues that God would have us see about himself. It will also take time to fully develop, and as more questions arise, there will be a greater need to study and understand the concept as a whole. Each time a new definition is provided or explained, it must then be tested through all the other doctrines. There will be times when the explanation is considered a good fit, and other times it will be seen that the definition leads to heresy, and the church as a whole often decides which is which.

This study will help in advancing the knowledge of who God is and how He wants His people to know Him. The historical underpinnings help to prevent the repetition of bad decisions and build on the good doctrines tested through time. The Trinitarian God is a compilation of many biblical references that lead to this very important doctrine.[94] The church leaders in the first couple of centuries did not have a lot to say about the Trinity proper, possibly due to the fact that people did not see a need to even look for a definition. The world at the time was against the spread of the gospel, and the desire to stay alive often overshadowed thinking about the deep thoughts of Scripture. The most devoted preachers and teachers of the day were probably focused on basic theology. The basic theology, those that were more clearly laid out in Scripture, like God is loving and just. These and every other doctrine discussed ideas of the Trinity, but it is not the full process of trying to get all the pieces to work together. A great persecution of the church was in every corner of the world. This led to the spreading of the gospel because the people were being forced to scatter. Another possibility of why the Trinity was not an issue might be that there was agreement on the subject and not much needed to be said. In the first and second centuries, only a few church fathers even mentioned the concept of the Trinity. In Holmes's *Martyrdom of Polycarp,* he tells us that as Polycarp was being martyred, his last words were a prayer. He closed his prayer to God the Father, through the eternal and heavenly High Priest, Jesus Christ, and with the Holy Spirit, both now and for the ages to come.[95] Although he never mentioned the direct relationships to each other, he did give a hint as to how one is to pray and the beginning of an understanding of the Trinity.

Though not much was discussed about the Trinity, we do know that there was a wide affirmation of the early church by looking at the baptismal formula, Scriptures on prayer, and how to worship. Ecclesiology and apologetics also mentioned the concepts found in the Trinity. There were times when someone would begin a

---

94 Grudem, 226
95 Gregg R. Allison, Historical Theology: An Introduction to Christian Doctrine (Grand Rapids: Zondervan, 2011), 233

formulation of thought concerning the Trinity, but there were not a lot of early leaders who disagreed on this subject; therefore, not much can be found. There were times when a section of the Trinity was discussed, like when Hippolytus outlined the economy of the three as he looked over the first chapter of John. He stated that the Father is above all, the Son is through all, and the Holy Spirit is in all. He was the first to distinguish the function of persons as a functional relationship. He distinguished the persons by their roles or activities on earth.[96]

The doctrine of the Trinity had a slow development over many years. Starting in the beginning, there were all three persons actively involved in creation, but it was overlooked because God has one essence, and "In the beginning God created."[97] He is singular. Scripture tells us in Deuteronomy 6:4 that there is one God. No one was looking for three persons until Jesus came in the New Testament and claimed to be God. Then people started to logically consider how this could be. Looking back to Polycarp, it is hard to imagine that he was trying to be the first person to teach a new doctrine as he was getting ready to die. He was simply stating a practical reality of each of the persons as he saw them in their various roles. Polycarp advanced the thought even without trying. This doctrine moved slowly because at the beginning it was not the intent to explain a new doctrine per se, but it was to explain a part of the doctrine that dealt with another area, thus advancing the theology of both.

As each new concept is introduced, the surrounding circumstances and the historical realities of the theologian will affect how and why the new teachings are introduced. Modern theologians will need to take into account the historical realities facing the writer. Modern theologians will also have their own surroundings to acknowledge and

---

96 Ibid, 234.
97 Gn 1:1

know that future theologians will judge their work in the same way, or they may judge today's decisions on criteria that have yet to be introduced.

CHAPTER 7
Historical Controversies

Historical controversies happen in the moments of time when someone has considered a new concept that challenges or adds to orthodox teaching, where two or more parties are not in agreement. The first controversy regarding the Trinity started around A.D. 200 with the Gnostics. The Gnostics introduced Monarchianism to the church. This is from the words *mono,* meaning one, and *archa,* the root meaning chief. The first form of Monarchianism stated, "All reality manifests a particular mode of God."[98] This form of Monarchianism would be described by the analogy of a stone being thrown into a pond. The center is the core being of God. There is an emanation from the core like the waves. The further out, the weaker it is and the less God-like it is. They would describe God as having different layers and different levels of gods.[99] This new view was not only anti-Trinitarian, but it was against any concept of God that had been previously discussed. The idea was to keep God as far away from matter as possible, and any idea of Jesus would have to limit Him to the spiritual only. It would be closer to describing pantheism, everything is God, and there are various levels of perfection. Making it a hierarchy of God. Some things are closer to being fully God than others. The question remains, how is that determined?

98Sproll, 2.55min.
99 Ibid, 5:20.

Origen was the first to address the Gnostic error of their false doctrine. In response to this controversy, he inserted the word hypostases into the definition of the persons of the Trinity. He stated that they were one in essence but three in person. He also stated that the Holy Spirit has always been and was not created.[100] Just as the Son was before, the Holy Spirit can be seen throughout Scripture and never came into being. He is outside of time as we know it. Origen also rejected the Gnostics on their speculation on how the world was created. He reaffirmed that the apostles taught that Jesus Christ is the Son of God, begotten before all of creation, and while becoming human, He remained divine. He also affirmed that the Holy Spirit's glory is no less than that of the Father and the Son.[101] Glory is another characteristic identified here, but would be found in the holiness section of this work. The glory is seen in the essence of God and is located within each person. Origen was a faithful apologist in this respect, but he also would not completely be orthodox in many of his writings on the Trinity. He did feel a connection to the people in the Monarchianism movement that he argued against. This is where the reader needs to take caution. No one gets everything right all the time, and with Origen, it is with the Trinity that he got a little correct and a lot wrong. We should always take caution with new concepts, and the reader should not assume someone is always right or always wrong. All arguments need to be tested. Just remember, when panning for gold, you have to wash out all the dirt to get the gold. Origen left a lot of dirt in his theology, but some of his first thoughts are worth mentioning. At the same time, the dirt must be seen as well, so it can be dooly discarded and called out as bad teaching.

---

100 Allison, 237.
101 Justo L. Gonzalez, The Story of Christianity Vol 1, (New York: Harper Collins, 1984), 1 79.

Origen went too far when He was trying hard to help distinguish the persons of the Trinity. He began a new view that became known as Subordinationism. This was where the Son was of the same nature, was eternal and divine, but still not equal to the Father in being or attributes. The Son was subordinate and inferior to the Father. This was close to many of the ideas considered orthodox in modern times, but to add that Jesus was inferior to the Father takes away the deity of Christ.[102] This would be condemned in the first church council. It is often the case in studying the Trinity that to defend one part well ends up tarnishing another part. Often, the tarnished part becomes known as heretical, and the whole of the person's argument is dismissed. A.H. Strong clarified this thought and agreed that the Son was subordinate to the Father, but He was also equal, not inferior, to the Father. He suggests that the priority is not superiority. It is a subordination of order, office, and operation, not in essence.[103] Strong suggests that Origen had many parts correct, but there was a great need to fix the issue of the subordination of Christ.

Origen had issues following the people of his day and desired to find commonality with those seemingly opposed to his views. Origen believed in two creations. This might have been a popular view at the time, but it was never considered orthodox. At the fall of humanity to sin, he stated that those who fell the furthest became demons, and the ones who fell a little had to have flesh.[104] This would play well for the Gnostics of his day, but it is not helpful today in the defense of the faith in the creation story. Not finding any Scripture reference for Origen's view, one can only speculate on his reasoning for a second creation. Origen, like most of us, had his good thoughts and his bad ones. In the case of debates and relationships, it is often hard to

---

102 Grudem, 245
103 Ibid, 252
104 Ibid, p. 79

separate the two. As a debater, winning the argument is the main goal, but at the end of the day, you can see the point of view of the other side. Their valid arguments would make one consider accepting their full point of view. Here, Origen seems to be holding a biblical view to start, but was willing to compromise on other issues. It also shows that one area of misunderstanding, like making Jesus not only subordinate to the Father but inferior, disqualifies Jesus from being of one essence with the Father and thereby not God. This disqualifies Jesus from being the savior and unravels salvation as it is taught in the New Testament. One word too far sets off an avalanche of false teaching. Be cautious!

A form of Monarchianism that helped change the early 200s A.D. was Modalistic Monarchianism. The chief leader of this view was Sabellius. Many times, this idea is called Sabellianism after its namesake. Sabellius proposed an analogy stating that God was like the sun and its rays. The rays partake and are of the same essence as the sun. In this case, Jesus is like the rays.[105] Clearly, this was his way to demonstrate how God could be one, but seen as three. The problem of making a mystery into something simple is that a mystery is still unknown on the human side of the relationship. It will be seen that each time someone tries to use an analogy, like the one here, something within the easy description will be wrong. Sabellius believes that the Son participates as the deity but is acting as a mode of God. God acts as the Father in one place and then the Son at another. Then God the Holy Spirit is introduced after Jesus returns to heaven. It has already been shown that the Holy Spirit was with Mary before Jesus was conceived. Even if Sabellius is willing to see them come and go, they are together at Mary's visit with Elizabeth, who was pregnant with John the Baptist. If God is only in one mode at a time, how is Jesus alive in Mary and the Spirit Moving in Elizabeth

---

105 Sproll, 9:43 min.

and John the Baptist? Sabellius is trying to show that God is the mode in which He presently shows Himself. He is not three persons but one being showing Himself in different modes. On its face, this is shown to be a false teaching.

With the exception of the above, most of the disputes were seemingly small and were among the local body of priests and bishops. The first person to pen a definition for the Trinity was Tertullian around 200A.D. He was writing against Praxeas, an unknown bishop, some believed he was the Roman bishop using a pseudonym. Tertullian was also the one who coined the phrase "one substance and three persons."[106] The understanding of the Trinity in the first and second centuries came about with the early church holding to the definition of monotheism and trying to incorporate their high view of Christology into the formula. The difficulty with such criteria is keeping an even balance of all three persons. Since they were open about the fact that they wanted to emphasize the Son, the overemphasis should be looked at closely.

Tertullian looked at Genesis 1:26 and noted the plural form for us. Let "us" make man in "our" image.[107] Many scholars want to say the plural form was just a way to say a royal we, and the singular form should be observed. The reason to argue for this would be to keep monotheism paramount. Research has proved otherwise; it shows that there are only two instances of royalty using the "we" form in ancient writings. Alexander the Great and King Demetrius did use the royal "we"; however, both were in Greek and never in Hebrew. They too were in 152-145B.C. and were too far removed from the Genesis writing to be compared. Only the Babylonian Talmud would give any consideration to this form of "we" in the Hebrew language. This, too,

---

106 Gonzalez, Vol. 1., 77.
106 Allison, 236.

does not make the Psalm 45 or Genesis 1 passages applicable.[108] There just does not seem to be any use of the "we" in a singular form before 152 B.C., making it implausible that this would be the accepted use of we. With all the other writings being void of this use, it is not a natural occurrence. Let alone in two different places that seem to be showing a plurality, not a royal single position. This does not disprove monotheism within scripture, but forces the theologian to look at the picture in a different way.

Tertullian held to monotheism and wrote against the thought of God showing Himself in three separate modes. He would argue against statements like, sometimes God would be the Father, then God would show himself as the Son, and then the Son would send the Holy Spirit. The main problem with Praxeas and earlier with Sabellius was their misuse or ignoring of passages like Mark 1:9-12. The Father speaks, the Son is baptized, and the Holy Spirit takes the Son away to the temptation. There is no way that all three could be doing their job and yet just be a mode of one God at the same time. The oneness of God is a very important part of who God is, but it cannot be ignored that there are three persons in the Trinity.

Tertullian was the first church father to use Latin in his writings.[109] In his use of Latin, he drew from legal terms that God was one in substance and three in persons.[110] Marcion, a contemporary of Tertullian, was a brilliant thinker who denied that the Father of Jesus was identical with the God of the Old Testament. He disparaged all things material, as did the Gnostics. Marcion could not grasp the full nature of God, and so his logical thought was that if God is Spirit and it was creation that fell due to sin, then all things created were affected by the fall. That must mean that all things made are evil. With God

---

108 Grudem, 227.
109 Gonzalez, 77.
110 Ibid, 77.

being Spirit from John 4, then God remains in the spiritual realm only. This helps him keep the Old and New Testaments separated. It was this heresy that led the church to study these beliefs and the acceptance of the unity of the Old and New Testaments, as well as creation and redemption being resolved by the church. It was during the exchanges of Tertullian and Marcion that the word "trinitas" was coined. Tertullian stated, "We do not worship three gods, for each of the divine persons is 'one substance' una substantia."[111] The differences of opinion would have to be hammered out at the next council.

Plato, who lived a couple of centuries before Christ, was the one who taught that there is a difference between essence, existence, and subsistence. Plato explained that to have essence meant that you were non-changing and would not change. To be in existence meant that you had the potential to change, and each day was different with new potential. Subsistence will be looked at later, but it says that something is standing under another.[112] The third definition will be addressed later, but it does not show that any part of God is under in being. The word usage for subsistence used by Tertullian is with the understanding of the persons in the Trinity and how they relate to one another, not in their relation to being. It will be shown that Tertullian does come back to this word when helping explain the relationship of the persons in the Trinity in the next section. Jesus is the same yesterday, today, and forever.[113] This helped Tertullian conclude that Jesus could not change, but also that he will not change. This helps to see that God does not merely exist at the moment. God is therefore "essence."[114] Tertullian also used these definitions to define the persons of the Godhead. He used the word "personi" to distinguish the

---

111 Daniel L. Akin, A Theology for the Church. (Nashville: B & H Publishing Group, 2007), 211.
112 Sproll, 8:14min.
113 Heb. 13:8.
114 Sproll, video 13:30min.

persons of the Trinity.[115] This is the use of subsistence in describing the persons, and essence is used for the whole of God.

It was during the years of Tertullian that Sabellianism came to a point of greatest controversy. Sabellius was a well-liked member of the clergy and had a great following. By the definitions used in their arguments, one of these two men had to be wrong and therefore heretical. When at a crossroads in belief, heresy forces the church to be precise and define what is truth as well as what is false and harmful to the body.[116] This is why the bishops in the Christian world gathered from around the known world in Antioch in 267A.D. It was here that the bishops decided to use the term, homousious to explain how we understand the essence of God. This is the word defined as being of the same substance as the Father.[117] Homousious helped determine for the people that God the Father and the Son were of the same substance and introduced plurality and division into the persons of the Trinity.[118] God was not one being just using different modes of expression, but three in person. The Father, the Son, and the Holy Spirit have the same essence.

For several generations, the Christian world seemed to be at peace with the decision of the council. There were almost one hundred years between the first minor controversy stated above and the second, much larger controversy concerning the Trinity. Another form of Monarchianism arrived within the church in the early 300s. Dynamic Monarchianism was about preserving monotheism and giving the person of Christ priority. This is the same place where the first controversy started. The issue was that in this controversy, the high view of the Son from the orthodox teaching was challenged. This

---

115 Ibid, 3:25min.
116 Ibid, 3:45 min.
117 Akin , 212.
118 Ibid, 212.

unbalanced understanding of the Son became a huge problem for the church for many years. Dynamic Monarchianism originated with Theodotus in Rome but was spread by the bishop of Antioch. They both believed that the power of the Son was given to a man named Jesus by God the Father at His baptism. Jesus was just an ordinary man who was a really good person who was considered holy by God, but He was not God.[119] Yes, the leading spiritual leader of a major city taught that Jesus was not God, and many followed his teaching. The man who became the spokesperson for this thought was Arius of Alexandria, and the movement soon took on his name, Arianism.[120] Arius studied the passages of John 1 and Hebrews 1 and determined that these passages had Jesus being begotten. The conclusion was that if Jesus was begotten, He must be a created being. They also taught that it is through God's creation of the Son that the world was created and is not eternal. This view can be hard to follow, with Jesus being adopted by the Father at baptism, and the Son was created by the Father to create the universe, and the two were not one until the baptism of Jesus. He was adopted by God, and Christ was homousious to the Father but was not God.[121] He was using the term from the first council in Antioch, but was changing the meaning of the word. The discussion that started the whole controversy began in one church where the priest, Arius, was opposed to his bishop. Arius was a very charismatic and popular priest, and many people followed his teachings. Alexander, the bishop of Alexandria, was determined not to let him continue in this heresy. Alexander condemned Arius and removed him from his post as a priest. Arius did not accept his punishment and helped form protests and marches in the city. He believed that with his popularity, Alexander would have no choice but to retain him. His assumptions were correct, and the bishops and

---

119 Allison, 235.
120 Sproll, 16:40min.
121 Ibid 16:40min.

priests demanded that Alexander give him back his position and declare that he was wrong to dismiss Arius.[122] It was during this time that the Roman ruler, Constantine, defeated Licinius and consolidated the two empires. Having accepted Christianity as his own religion, Constantine became involved in the unrest in Alexandria. The debate became so heated that Constantine, the ruler of the western world, decided to first send his advisor to the city and come back with a recommendation. The report given stated that there was no hope for reconciliation. Constantine felt that this was important enough for the state to intervene for national security.[123] This would be the first church council to be convened by a ruler of the state. Constantine paid for all the bishops in the empire to come and decide the church's official understanding of the Trinity.[124] The state, having a vested interest in the decision of this council, would play a huge part in the church in years to come, both monetarily and through enforcement.

The largest question proposed to the council was: Is the Word of God co-eternal with God? Arius and his followers were saying, "There was when He was not." The word was not God, but He was the first of creation.[125] As you can see from the beginning of the argument, the council that was called by the emperor was for bishops only. The enormous cost of travel expenses would preclude many who wanted to debate this topic from coming, not to mention the space it would take to hold such a meeting. The church had already set up a hierarchical structure, so it was decided that those who had the rank of bishop or higher would be invited. All others would need to send their messages to a bishop to be considered. Arius, the main advocate of the view named after him, was just a priest and was not invited to sit on the council. He was left to give other bishops his arguments to

---

122 Gonzalez, 162.
123 Ibid, 162.
124 Ibid, 159-161.
125 Ibid, 161.

address the body of his work. They would have to present the argument and come up with their own answers to the opponent's questions, while Alexander of Alexandria was invited to the council and could argue for his case using his own thoughts and rebut any argument that needed rebuffing. The council was scheduled to be held in Nicea in A.D. 325. This council was called to determine the orthodox view of the Trinity, and to clear up any other issues that the bishops wanted to present for consideration.

All bishops were invited to the council, and not all were going to come, having just the two main positions that historians point out in their writings. The council was called to decide on an issue, not to vote between two possibilities. There were several subgroups of bishops that attended the council. The first was a small number of convinced Arians, who were led by Eusebius of Nicomedia. He was voted their chief spokesperson. Alexander of Alexandria led a small group that believed that Arius threatened the very core of Christianity. Most of the Latin bishops believed that Tertullian was enough and nothing more needed to be said, so they did not come to argue a point, but rather to argue not to argue. A small group of two or three wanted to defend the oneness of Father and Son so much that they were willing to have a new view called Patripassianism. This was the view that the Father was on the cross as well as the Son. However, the vast majority of the bishops attending did not have a set opinion when they arrived.[126]

As the great council of Nicea was formed, there were approximately 300 bishops from all over the empire in attendance. It took several months to seat the gathering because the empire was so vast and travel took some months to arrive. Many were from Spain, and others came from Africa. With the history of the empire changing

---

126 Ibid, 163-164.

hands in many areas, many of these bishops had been through torture and exile many times in their ministry. They knew what the consequences would be for those on the opposing side of the decision. These large issues would affect not just the teaching of the church, but they could also change many of the bishops' lives. Some may find themselves out of a job or exiled or even tortured. There were also smaller issues to be solved, like who to let back into the church after persecution, and how to elect and ordain elders and priests in the local church.[127] This is important because each of these special meetings would place a good number outside the church, and knowing what it took to be restored might help with the evaluation of their future votes.

The bishops understood that all their decisions would inevitably lead to one side being declared heretical, and some form of punishment was on the horizon. In the Trinity case, it seemed that both sides of the argument could not be right, but they could both be wrong. The majority of the bishops came to the meeting thinking that no decision at all would be best. If there are no set practices, then there would be freedom to do as they wished, and no punishment would be handed down by the winning side. However, the political leaders, who paid for the council to convene, knew that the people needed direction and political unrest would continue without a word from the church leaders. A no-decision was not an option, due to the political pressure applied; therefore, the bishops would have to come to a conclusion. They did not go into the council lightly. They too knew that if this matter was settled once and for all, persecution would be reduced overall, because everyone would know orthodoxy on these issues.

As the council came to the debate on the Trinity, it became Alexander's turn. One of the main arguments against the Arian view was that his view would leave the church with a Christ who was not

---

127 Ibid, 162-163.

worthy to be worshiped. If Jesus was not divine, and from our definition earlier, eternal, then He could not be considered of the one essence of God, and it would be idolatrous to worship Him.[128] Then, on turning to their positive argument, the Alexandrian position stated that the Son of the Heavenly Father was begotten from all eternity. He did not come to be at a point in time. He is eternal. There never was a time He was not. The Father and the Son have a relationship of total and mutual self-giving.[129] They quickly pointed out that if Jesus was created and not fully God, then how could a creature bear the full wrath of God for the sins of the people? If Jesus was just a created being, then no matter how good He was, He was not to be worshiped. However, the Bible tells us that He is to be worshiped in Philippians 2:9-11 and Revelation 5:12-14, just to mention two references.[130]

Then it would be Eusebius of Nicomedia's turn to speak. He believed that a simple logical argument would win the day, and this would be a short meeting. He was right in that his argument would shorten the meeting. After presenting a few minutes of his debate, the bishops stood up and shouted him down. His speech was snatched from his hand, torn to pieces, and then trampled underfoot. They also rejected that the Father and the Son were on the cross together, as the other group had proposed.[131] This was undoubtedly very embarrassing for this small group, and the aftermath of this decision would be felt greatly for years.

The council believed that they must be clear in their rejection of Arius. They first turned to scripture, but then felt a creed needed to be used to have a greater understanding of this theology. It was decided that Constantine's suggestion of homoousios would be used when

---

128 Akin, 212.
129 Ibid, 213
130 Grudem, 247.
131 Gonzalez, 165.

talking about the substance of God.[132] It was determined that the substance of God the Father and the Son were the same. The Nicene Creed would be the statement of faith for the church, and most modern church denominations still hold to its teachings.

We believe in one Lord Jesus Christ, the only begotten Son of God. Begotten of His Father before all the worlds, God of God, Light of Light, very God of very God, begotten, not made, being of one substance with the Father.[133]

The Nicene Creed is the most universally accepted Christian creed to this day. The Roman Catholics, Protestants, Greek Orthodox, and Russian Orthodox churches are in agreement with its teaching.[134] This, by no means, made things settled on the issue. Just as Arius did not like the ruling of his bishop, he did not like the ruling of the council.

The man who came out of the Nicene Council, who would become the leader of the council's defense and creed for years to come, was Athanasius. At the time of the great Council, he was only 29 and was invited as a secretary to Alexander, the bishop of Alexandria. He was not a bishop and had no say in the proceedings, but what he observed in the meetings changed his life forever. Just four years later, at the age of 33, he became the bishop of Alexandria. This is the same area that Arius was from, and it would be Athanasius who would have to defend the faith close to home. It is believed that he single-handedly kept the church from pagan intellectualism.[135]

---

132 Ibid, 165.
133 Akin, 212.
134 Gonzalez, 165.
135 Grudem, 245.

As Athanasius was becoming a leader for those adopting the Nicene Creed, Arius was discovering that the decision to have a great council was not that of the church or the bishops, but the bidding of the emperor. Arius and his followers soon realized that if you can persuade the political ruler to come your way, you will have the upper hand. Their plan took time, but it eventually worked. Constantine switched sides in the debate and, through a decree, was going to remove Athanasius from being a bishop. By A.D. 353, a pro-Arian policy was established and the entire kingdom was to follow the Dynamic Monarchianism model. Arius was good at persuading people that Athanasius's view held that there was no distinction between the Father and the Son. They used the homoousios, of the same substance, from the Creed to mean something different than what he believed. [136] It seems like a modern concept to just change the definition of a word if you do not like how it is used, but for almost two thousand years, men have simply changed the definition of well-established words to have the definition mean something new to the listener.

The new discussion came down to being able to see the difference between a distinction and a separation. R. C. Sproul described it like this. You can see this in the physical distinction of your physical and non-physical body. If I distinguish that you have a body and a soul, you are understood, but if I separate your body and your soul, you have been killed.[137] This understanding of distinction and separation will come into play with the Son and His nature in the 5th century as well.

A synod was gathered in Alexandrea to come to a resolution on the meaning of this argument in A.D. 362. At the conclusion of the synod, it was decided: "Father, Son, and Holy Spirit as one

136 Gonzalez, 178.
137 Sproul, 10:30min.

'substance' as long as this was not understood as obligating the distinction among the three. Three substances, as long as you do not see three gods."[138] Athanasius referred to Jesus and the Holy Spirit as consubstantial and homoousios, of one and the same substance with the Father. Yet the three are eternally distinct.[139] The Athanasian Creed is considered one of the benchmarks for the church today. It was this Creed that has given us a standard that has guided the church through the centuries. The part concerning the Trinity begins with statement three and concludes with the Trinity at twenty-nine, where it transitions into the person of the Son.

1. And the Catholic Faith is this: That we worship one God in Trinity, and Trinity in Unity;

2. Neither confounding the Persons, nor dividing the Substance.

3. For there is one Person of the Father: another of the Son: and another of the Holy Spirit.

4. But the Godhead of the Father, of the Son, and of the Holy Spirit, is all one: the Glory equal, the Mystery coeternal.

5. Such as the Father is, such is the Son: and such is the Holy Spirit.

6. The Father uncreated: the Son uncreated: the Holy Spirit uncreated.

7. The Father incomprehensible: the Son incomprehensible: and the Holy Spirit incomprehensible.

8. The Father eternal: the Son eternal: the Holy Spirit eternal.

9. And yet they are not three Eternals, but one eternal.

---

138 Gonzalez, 179.
139 Allison, 239.

10. And also, there are not three uncreated, nor three incomprehensibles, but one uncreated, and one incomprehensible.

11. So likewise, the Father is Almighty: the Son is Almighty: and the Holy Spirit is Almighty.

12. And yet they are not three Almighties, but one Almighty.

13. So the Father is God: the Son is God: and the Holy Spirit is God.

14. Yet they are not three Gods, but one God.

15. So likewise, the Father is Lord: the Son Lord: and the Holy Spirit Lord.

16. And yet not three Lords, but one Lord.

17. For as we are compelled by the Christian verity, to acknowledge every Person by himself to be God and Lord.

18. So we are forbidden by the Catholic Religion to say, There be three Gods or three Lords.

19. The Father is made of none: neither created nor begotten.

20. The Son is of the Father alone: not made, nor created, but begotten.

21. The Holy Spirit is of the Father and of the Son: neither made, nor created, nor begotten, but proceeding.

22. So there is one Father, not three Fathers: one Son, not three Sons: one Holy Spirit, not three Holy Spirits.

23. And in this Trinity none is afore, or after another: none is greater, or less than another.

24. But the whole three Persons are coeternal and coequal.

25. So that in all things, as aforesaid: the Unity in Trinity, and the Trinity in Unity, is to be worshipped.

26. He, therefore, who will be saved, must think of the Trinity.

27. Furthermore, it is necessary for everlasting salvation that he also believe rightly the Incarnation of our Lord, Jesus Christ.[140]

1. And the Catholic Faith is this: That we worship one God in Trinity, and Trinity in Unity;

In point three, it begins with the phrase "And the catholic faith is." It should be understood that the word catholic here has the definition of universal faith or the church at large. This is not the Roman Catholic Church or the denomination of a specific group. As a whole, the bishops were trying to convey that the following documents were to be considered orthodox by every Christian. It would be assumed that all Christians throughout the world would accept these basic teachings as foundational. This document is not a set of statements that were new to the church, nor were they seen as controversial. These statements were well-thought-out beliefs that all clergy could teach in good faith. Obviously, there were groups that did not like or adhere to some of the statements. It is because of these groups that the council found the need to publicly state that what follows should now be the norm for church belief and teaching. If a group could not hold to these teachings, then they are probably not Christians per point 29.

The first doctrinal statement in point three is that God is to be worshiped. This statement goes much further than just acknowledging God as the creator or sustainer. We are to give our full allegiance and love to the one God in Trinity. The word "in Trinity" here helps the Christian see that although we worship one God, He is special and as

---

140 Grudem, 1170-1171.

a greater being that cannot be fully understood. This special Trinity form of God shows that true unity is possible and practiced by all three. God is a jealous God, but He is not jealous of Himself. Within His unity, all three persons work in a very special way, demonstrating better than we can fathom the perfect cohesion of thought and action.

2. Neither confounding the Persons, nor dividing the Substance.

The fourth point simply explains how the individual members are to be recognized. The second definition in the Webster's dictionary for the word, confounding is most likely the definition for this passage. The definition shows that confounding is a mix-up with something else, so that the individual elements become difficult to distinguish.[141] The key is distinguishing the persons. The Father sends the Son,[142] the Son gives His life as a ransom,[143] and the Holy Spirit will convict people of their sin.[144] It can be seen how the parts of salvation are distinguished by the persons; however, it is not easy to distinguish how God the Father is one with the Son. Then Jesus tells the Christian, just as I and the Father are one, you should be one with me.[145] How does that work? It is sometimes easy to see the roles of the persons, but often it is hard to see. In Psalm 139, is it the Father or the Holy Spirit speaking to the Psalmist? The key is found in the second half of four. Great caution should be exercised not to separate the persons into their own being. There must be no separation of the unity of God. He is one and always will be one.

3. For there is one Person of the Father: another of the Son: and another of the Holy Spirit.

---

141 Websters dictionary, Confounded
142 1 Jn 4:14
143 Mt. 20:28
144 Jn 16:8
145 Jn 10:30

Number five in the statement is a continuation of number four. There is only one being and one essence of God. With this, we can further investigate that God is three in person. His distinguishing functions are seen in relationships. In a perfect world, fathers are understood to have a function of support, wisdom, and understanding toward their children. Sons in this world try to live up to the lessons and direction of their father. Sons will also emulate the life of the father. This world can be seen in the demonstration of how God shows His love for us. The relationship God gives is in the concept of His distinguished persons. The Holy Spirit also shows that even within His name, Spirit, He adds another dimension that is outside the relationship that man naturally looks for. The person of the Holy Spirit will be explored further in this book.

4. But the Godhead of the Father, of the Son, and of the Holy Spirit, is all one: the Glory equal, the Mystery coeternal.

Number six is coming back once again to the wholeness of the single God. Each of the three has His responsibilities, but in the end, they all share the same glory. This concludes with the answer to one of the great dilemmas. The Trinity is seen as a mystery. This was fully discussed previously as knowledge that God has that people cannot fully explain. The part not to overlook is that God has always been together in complete unity. The "forever" in the statement also gives us great relief to know there is more to life than we will ever see here, and He is in control and can see it all from His perspective.

5. The Father uncreated: the Son uncreated: the Holy Spirit uncreated.

Statement number seven has been at the center of many controversies through the years. Many have been discussed in this section. On its face, it seems easy to understand, but there have been many church leaders who look at the Son as the first of creation, having been begotten. They look at passages like John 3:16 and conclude that begotten means created, or had a starting point post the existence of the Father. This leads to a very large problem philosophically. If the Trinity is in universal Unity, then all three persons must be tied together eternally, and the Unity cannot come anytime the other was not. To claim that the Son had a beginning is stating that He cannot be God, because He does not meet the qualifications of being eternal in essence. This discussion will be fully addressed in the person of the Son in a later section, but if all three are God, then they are all the causal agents of all creation.

6. The Father incomprehensible: the Son incomprehensible: and the Holy Spirit incomprehensible.

The number nine statement parallels the number six statement regarding the mystery of the Trinity. There is no easy way to explain God. Almost every time someone tries to explain the Trinity by giving an analogy, it is almost always laced with some form of heresy.[146] It would just be easier for people to say we will never understand God and acknowledge He is incomprehensible in all His being; however, there is a reason to pursue an understanding of God. God is relational in how he works with each person of the Trinity, and He is relationship-minded toward His people. If we are to be as one with the Father as Jesus was one with the Father, then we should do our best to understand Him. Part of a relationship with other people is getting to know them better. Even though God is incomprehensible, it is still our responsibility to build on what is understandable.

7. The Father eternal: the Son eternal: the Holy Spirit eternal.

8. And yet they are not three Eternals, but one eternal.

---

146 House, H. Wayne. Charts of Christian Theology and Doctrine: Zondervan, Nashville, 1992 p.50

Points ten and eleven go together in understanding the way God is eternal. Taking this into account with God being omni-present demonstrates just how awe-inspiring God really is. The first statement demonstrates that God in all three persons is eternal, but He is also eternal in the one being. God has had an infinite amount of time without creation, and an infinite time with His creation. God was fully satisfied with His relationship without people and did not have to have creation to be fulfilled. However, He created people to have relationships with other people, and they are to have a relationship with God. He desired to give people one of His characteristics, that of relationship. In His eternal nature, He is complete and fully satisfied.

9. So likewise, the Father is Almighty: the Son is Almighty: and the Holy Spirit is Almighty.

10. And yet they are not three Almighties, but one Almighty.

Points twelve and thirteen show the attribute also known as omnipotence. He is all powerful, and within the workings of the godhead, each person and the essence of God can do any act within the overall character of God. If there is anything God cannot do, then there is something more powerful, and the most powerful would be worthy of worship. At this point, I will not delve into the absurdity of questions like, Can God sin? Questions like this would distract from the point and not be helpful in understanding the Trinity. For the purposes here, God can do anything that does not violate His nature and characteristics.

11. So the Father is God: the Son is God: and the Holy Spirit is God.

12. Yet they are not three Gods, but one God.

13. So likewise, the Father is Lord: the Son Lord: and the Holy Spirit Lord.

14. And yet not three Lords, but one Lord.

15. For as we are compelled by the Christian verity, to acknowledge every Person by himself to be God and Lord.

So we are forbidden by the Catholic Religion to say, There be three Gods or three Lords.

These statements take on the very reason we study the Trinity. It is here that we answer the questions: Who is God? And how do we address Him? He is one God and Lord. He has total jurisdiction, and Christians must give Him our very lives. He is seen as the one God of Israel that is also God the Father, God the Son, and God the Holy Spirit. All of which are God, and all are to be Lord. Each of these correlates with salvation. The "lordship" of Jesus in Romans 10:9 makes it clear that Jesus must be made Lord for salvation to happen. These statements go even further to say that the Lordship of all three persons is so tightly bound that the Christian must also accept the Father and the Holy Spirit as Lord, just as the Son is made Lord in the person's profession. It is just as clear in this section that to make just one Lord is not only un-Christlike, but is forbidden by the universal church. All Christians should hold these beliefs, and if not, all Christians should keep such a person from teaching false doctrine. Point twenty-eight also makes this clear. The proper view of the Trinity is absolutely necessary for salvation.

There are even more parts to the creed that will not be specifically addressed in this section, but have been covered in the above paragraphs and in other parts of this book. It would behoove the reader to look at the whole of the creed and notice that the next section deals with Christology and how it relates to the Son, Jesus Christ.

The dating of this Creed cannot be determined, but it was credited to Athanasius. It was his beliefs and teachings that led to the next great council, which solidified much of what was used in the Second Ecumenical Council. This Council was to be called in the city of Constantinople in A.D. 381. Athanasius's death prior to the council's convening would force others to decide how the church would clear up the understanding of the Trinity.[147] The Council of Constantinople reworked the Nicaean Creed to make clearer the affirmation of the deity of both the Son and the Holy Spirit. Augustine of Hippo added a phrase that would later lead to a major rift in the catholic church. Until this time, it was understood that the Father is the one doing the sending of the Son and the Son sends the Spirit, but here we see that the Father and the Son send the Spirit. Hence, he added a double procession of the Spirit from Romans 8:9, and the other view held that the Holy Spirit is also from the Father.[148] From A.D.381 to A.D. 451, the basic view of the Trinity stood with little controversy. The disagreements started over the doctrine of the Son, which bled into the doctrine of the Trinity. Gregory of Nazianzus stated that if Adam's entire nature fell, all of Adam must unite with all of the Son in order for the whole of Adam to be saved.[149] This was the start of the controversy concerning how Jesus could be human and divine at the same time. Nestorius was the representative of the Antiochene school. He would soon be the bishop of Constantinople, and with this post, he would have a prestigious position. This caused a problem for Gregory because the last council had set up a hierarchy of bishops like the West, with Constantinople being the head. The Antiochene school wanted to change the language from Mary the mother of God to Mary the mother of Christ. This change was not about Mary; it was his way of stating who Christ is to us. Nestorius was declaring that in Jesus there were two natures and therefore there must be two persons. One was divine, and one was human. The human was born of Mary, but the divine was not. A council was called, and only half could get there in time.[150] Nestorius declared that he was correct when those who

---

147 Gonzalez, 185.
148 Grudem, 246.
149 Gonzalez, 253.
150 Ibid, 253-255.

were close in proximity to the council arrived and were more under Nestorius's influence. So when the other half arrived, they called their own council and denounced the first. Back and forth it went for many years.

The political leaders of the day could change not only the local governance, but it often changed the direction of all life, including the church. Pulcheria, the new empress, held a new council to meet in Chalcedon in A.D. 451. This was considered the Fourth Ecumenical Council. It was decided at the council that Nestorius was wrong and that Tertullian was correct in saying that Christ had two natures in one person.[151] Chalcedon is considered the terminal council of the Christian understanding of Christ. This meant that no other council would be called for the purpose of discussing the issue. This helps give clarity and a final verdict on our understanding of the Son. It was determined that Christ was *vera deus vera homo*. Jesus is truly God and truly man. He has two natures, one is fully human, and the other is fully divine.[152] The four points of the argument are that He is united without mixture, confusion, division, or separation. These boundaries were set with each nature retaining its own attributes.[153] The best way to look at this is to look at the death of Christ. As he is on the cross, we can see that He gives His spirit back to the Father and His body dies. Therefore, the human side of his nature died on the cross, and the God nature was still there.[154] Nestorianism was put to rest. The belief that two natures meant two persons was refuted.[155] This may have been the determining council for this issue, but as we have seen through these times of turbulence, it is never really over.

---

151 Ibid, 256
152 Sproll, 14:49min.
153 Ibid, 17:00 min.
154 Sproll, 12:08 min.
155 Ibid, 7:40 min.

As the East and West became further separated in politics, their councils too became separate. In A.D. 589, the third Council of Toledo (Spain) was held. They substituted one word in the Nicene Creed, *filioque*. This affirmation stated that the Holy Spirit proceeded from the Son and the Father. In 1274 A.D., at the Council of Lyons, it was reaffirmed for the Western churches. At that time, it was rejected by the East.[156]

An eastern bishop, Photius, in A.D. 867, declared that bishop Ignatius and the West were heretical because they misused the Nicene Creed. The Western churches had adopted the *filioque*. The phrase, "and from the Son," was added to the phrase of who sends the Holy Spirit. The original phrase was "from the Father, through the Son." When they added the new phrase, it became, "from the Father, and from the Son."

This argument over who was the sender of the Holy Spirit became one of three issues that split the East from the West. It looked as though the two could not come to terms. The Western church accepted the Apostles' Creed, clerical celibacy as a universal rule, and unleavened bread for communion. The East wanted to reconcile with the West, so an envoy from the West was sent to see if there was any room for compromise within the two systems. On June 16, 1054, a Roman Cardinal sent by the Pope came to Constantinople. As the spokesperson for the Pope, he attended the meetings with the Bishop of Constantinople. The Cardinal could not see that there could be an agreement, so he walked up to the altar of the Bishop's church, pronounced excommunication on the entire East, and walked out, dusting his shoes off at the door.[157] This would be the last time the church as a universal catholic church existed.

---

156 Allison, 243.
157 Gonzalez, 265.

The rationalist impulse of the medieval years had some priests taking the stance of tri-theism. Tri-theism denies that there is only one God, but rather argues that each of the Persons is an individual God. The belief was held by Roscellinus.[158] This belief was not widely held because it is very much polytheistic, and could not work with a unified being of God as one. There is no true unity, and with nothing holding it together, it becomes a mess quickly.[159] It also violated most of the Old Testament teachings that there is one God, like the verses in Deuteronomy 6.

Thomas Aquinas and other medieval philosophers applied three arguments during this time to describe God and who He was. The first argument was ontological and would then be an argument from His very existence. How can we know there is a God? It is because we know there must be something that first existed; therefore, by His existence as creator, He must be God. Having the idea of God implies the very existence of God. Its validity depends on whether existence can be taught as a predicate. The second is cosmological. What can be seen and known about God in the created order? Items like motion, cause and effect, necessary being, degrees of perfection, and purpose are examples of how God shows Himself. This shows us that God is, but it does not show us who God is. The last is the teleological argument that states that we can see God because of the "design" of the universe.[160] This form of argument comes out of science and observation. How can we prove God without the Bible? What form of observation will give us evidence that God exists? The scientific method of observation is utilized to make an intellectual determination as to the existence of God. Mathematical calculations on gravity, the speed of the rotation of the earth, the placement of the

---

158 Akin, 214.
159 Grudem, 248.
160 Akin, 215.

atmosphere, and the sun's location to earth are observations that show there was a creator with a design. One of these, just slightly adjusted, keeps people from living. This was their goal and method of questioning God.

Thomas Aquinas had applied philosophy to his traditional formulation with the notion of a person and relationships. He stated that it is subsistent with the divine essence. Meaning that the persons of the Trinity were standing under the whole of the essence of God, each fulfilling their assignments. This is the place where the definition of subsistence was introduced by Plato earlier in the book. The Father had a relationship by paternity to the Son. The Son had a relation to the Holy Spirit by *filiation*. The Father and Son had a relationship by giving the Holy Spirit, and the Holy Spirit proceeding from the Father and the Son had a relationship in return. They all have the same essence, or they would not be God.[161] It was during this time that external philosophy was seen as a greater tool than just using the Bible to understand God.

One last attempt to get the two parties of the church together again was at the Council of Florence in 1439 A.D. It started as a serious attempt by both sides, but after much debate, the three previous issues could not be reconciled, and the attempt failed.[162] The church has remained split to this day, with no attempt to reconcile. In less than another hundred years, an even greater split would occur in the West with the Protestant Reformation.

Most of the reasons concerning the Protestant Reformation did not have direct ties to the doctrine of the Trinity. It is believed that most of the theologians of the 1500s were all in agreement with the previous generations. Calvin believed that "The human mind is a factory of

---

161 Allison, 245.
162 Ibid, 245.

idols," and we can only know the true and living God when He chooses to reveal Himself to us in His Son, through His Word, and by His Spirit.[163] Martin Luther followed suit and was following the same path as his predecessors concerning the Trinity. He wrote, "We have had to use the word *person* just as the fathers also have used it, for we have no better term. It signifies nothing else than hypostasis."[164] The view of the Trinity would not be significantly challenged again for nearly 400 years. It would be in modern times that not only the Trinity would be challenged, but every doctrine of the Bible would be greatly debated.

---

163 Akin, 218.
164 Geisler, 274.

CHAPTER 8
Modern Controversy

In the age of enlightenment, everything religious came into question. Scholars in the modern period of the 1920s started to deemphasize the doctrine of the Trinity. It became so bad that Karl Rahner said that if we totally dropped the Trinity, religious literature would barely change.[165] People had all but taken God out of religion. It is amazing how centuries of teaching, debating, and sacrificing for the basic tenets of the faith could all be forgotten in such a short amount of time.

Liberal Protestantism had become the norm in the early 1900s, but one prominent theologian, Karl Barth, broke away from the others and began writing on multiple issues. In his book, *Church Dogmatics,* written and published from 1932-1967, he showed that the whole of a man's faith starts with God. He, like Paul House of the late 1900's early 2000's, placed the doctrine of the Trinity as the head of all dogmatics. Barth stated that the Trinity tells us who God is and must be the first topic discovered or studied at the outset. He is also credited with the idea of the social Trinity. God is the revealer, Jesus is the revelation, and the Holy Spirit is the revealdness.[166] Barth was not accepted by the liberals nor by the conservatives, but his willingness

---

165 Allison, 248.
166 Allison, 248-250.

to take a stand in his day is seen as one of the first moves back toward the historical beliefs of the Trinity.

Another of the modern scholars, Kevin Giles, denounced the eternal order in the Godhead. He believed that to elevate one person in the Trinity would automatically make one of the other person's inferior. This would make the Trinity not possible due to the persons not being of the same substance. J. Scott Horrell, on the other hand, supported the order of the Godhead and proposed an eternally ordered social model of the Trinity. He saw the Father having preeminence, the collaboration of the Son, and the activity of the Holy Spirit.[167] With the new thinking of equality for all, many scholars could not understand how the subsistence of the persons of God would work, and just dropped the idea. The misconceptions coming from this time not only changed how people understood God, but also changed how people related to other people. This would also later play into the sexual revolution and how one misunderstanding of God leads to a snowball effect of misunderstanding how we are to love and communicate.

One of the emerging groups that felt one person of the Trinity was overlooked was the "Oneness" Pentecostals. The idea of the Holy Spirit being seen as under the Father and Son was unacceptable, and because of this, the group denied the Trinity. The organization originated in the Assembly of God denomination. Their view became a modalistic view of God, and the Spirit is how He shows Himself today.[168] The new form of modalism was not keeping the oneness of God. It was on emphasizing the person of the Holy Spirit because they felt He was neglected.

---

167 Ibid, 252.
168 Allison, 252

However, the recent rise in Islam, Hinduism, and Buddhism has caused the Christian community to look at its own historical roots and discover that a return to its Trinitarian roots was logical and needed. They have found that it is their allegiance and worship of this God that has enhanced their life. It seems that the doctrine of the Trinity will take a primary place in the third millennium.[169] Only time will tell, but Jesus has told us that His church will prevail and will last all time.[170]

Putting the mystery together is still a task that we will not accomplish with an in-depth study, but there have been many advancements in knowing more of God. We start with knowing we have one God. "Listen, Israel: The Lord is our God, the Lord is one."[171] Secondly, we have several instances where the persons are all accounted for at one event, like Mark 1:10, "As soon as He came up out of the water, He saw the heavens being torn open and the Spirit descending to Him like a dove. And a voice came from heaven: You are My beloved Son; I take delight in You!" The words for the deity are found in the Father who is talking, the Son being baptized, and the Spirit that is coming down to the Son from the Father. There is no contradiction in these passages, but there is an enormous amount of relationship God is showing His people.

Consider the qualities associated with the relationship. Only within a relationship can God express interpersonal attributes such as love, sympathy, intimacy, self-giving, and communication. Only between distinct persons can there be giving and taking, initiating and responding, sharing and self-revelation, union and communion. For God to be fully personal, then, capable of love and community, there must be genuine plurality within the divine being itself. Historic

---

169 Allison, 253
170 Mt. 16:18.
171 Dt. 6:4.

Christian theology teaches that these interpersonal attributes were expressed from all eternity among the three Persons of the Trinity. In this way, Christianity is able to maintain within the Godhead the highest conception of what it means to be a personal being.[172]

A proper understanding of how the persons of the Trinity interact with each other will give a glimpse into their individual personal roles. A full study of the person of the Father, Son, and Holy Spirit will help humanity discover that the God of the universe wants that same relationship with His people, and He has made us in His image for just this reason. Not only does He desire this relationship, He was willing to send His Son to give us a chance to see how it is supposed to work.

No other world religion has a concept of the Trinity in its teachings. The Jewish people only acknowledge one God, and they do not accept the Son or the Spirit as part of the Godhead. The Muslims only have one god, and their god cannot be interpersonal because, as he is described, he cannot logically have that ability. And other pantheistic cultures do not accept that they are in any way unified; if anything, they are at odds with one another. The Trinity in His form and function is very unique to the Christian worldview, and it lends itself to a philosophical argument that shows an in-depth thought process that for centuries has been debated. The uniqueness and complexity of the Trinity show that no man could or would come up with a system this complex and still have a thriving and functioning religion two thousand years later. This doctrine's explanation of who God is and how He functions tells the world just how special our God is.[173]

---

172 Nancy Pearcey, Finding Truth, (Colorado Springs: David C. Cook, 2015), 131.
173 Akin, 218.

CHAPTER 9
Three in Person

This new section is here to help us see that within the unity of the one essence of God, there are three distinguished persons. The Father, the Son, and the Holy Spirit each have the full qualities of God, and as seen in section one, they are of the same singular essence. In that section, it was the goal to identify if each person was of the one essence or being known as God. In the first section, it was seen that the oneness of God was established in a tight Unity and function.

This section will now look to distinguish the roles that each individual plays within the United God. With the three persons, Father, Son, and Holy Spirit, what are the expectations and functions that make the Father distinct from the others? It will be maintained that they are all God, but what makes each special, and how are we, as His creation, to relate to the individual persons discussed? The functions of the person will help us understand how to better relate to God and how He wishes us to address Him in our spiritual practices, like salvation and prayer.

CHAPTER 10
The Father as Person

The Father as a Person must be seen as a distinguished person in the Trinity, but not different in essence from the whole. This section will help discover the person of the Father as God and establish His roles as God. When studying the Father, it must be recognized that there is no separate section devoted to Him. Theology proper does discuss some of His functions, but it is based on the "being" of God. The study of theology proper is an overarching concept of God; however, the Father is the only person of the Trinity without a separate "ology." This makes distinguishing His characteristics all the more difficult. The approach taken here will be to look through scripture passages that help discover who the Father is and His relationship to the Trinity and mankind. It will be seen that His relationship with humanity is unique.

With the challenge of the person of the Father being the most difficult to research, it will be important to recognize His function in the scriptures, and from that point deduce His roles. When looking for the use of the term "father" in the concordance. It would seem that if the church saw the persons of the Trinity in the Bible, it would be common. The word for father in the Old Testament is not as common as one might think, so the first step is to look at the words associated with Father in the Old and New Testaments. The words then will need to be analyzed to see if they fit the Fatherhood of God as His character or just the title of a person.

The use of God the Father is surprisingly rare when looking at the Old Testament. There are plenty of references to how a father is to be in a relationship with others,[174] and there are references to His Fatherhood to the nations,[175] but using the word Father is not as common.[176] It is in His relationship to the Son in the New Testament that we see the greatest distinction of function. Therefore, we will look at the relationships that the Father has with His Son in the New Testament and then look at how His interactions with His Son correlate with how humans are to relate to the Father and what forms of relationship fathers are to have with their sons. The idea behind this section is to distinguish the person of the Father from the Son and the Holy Spirit. We are asking the question: What is it about the Father that is different than the other two?

Even when you are looking at the individual Persons of the Trinity, you will notice that the other two will be close by and working together to accomplish the task. As it would be expected, the unity of persons being in the same essence would always be working in tandem on everything. The Three are so close in relationship that even while distinguishing them, you will not want to separate them.

The person of the Father in Hebrews 1:1-3 tells us that God is the great architect of the universe.[177] In verse two, it shows that it is through the Son that the Father created everything for His glory, and it is through the Son that His glory is revealed to the people. The glory of the creation of the universe belongs to the Father. He is the ultimate person in the Trinity while remaining equal. The Son has the full glory

---

174 Gn. 27:34, Gn. 2:24, Pr. 29:3.
175 Dt. 32:6; Is. 63:16.
176 Robert Stein, "Fatherhood of God." http://www.biblestudytools.com /dictionaries/bakers-evangelical-dictionary/fatherhood-of-god.htm, (accessed August 8, 2016).
177 Bruce Ware, Father, Son, and Holy Spirit: Relationships, Roles and Relevance, (Wheaton: Crossway, 2005), 51.

of God, but Jesus is the perfect reflection of God's glory to the people. In Hebrews 1:3, the supremacy of the Father is made clear when it states that Christ returns to heaven and is given the great honor of the right hand of the Father. Therefore, the one with great power and authority is the Father. For example, one cannot stand at the right of the king and claim to be the king. There is only one majesty sitting on the throne of heaven. This in no way states that the equality of the Son is less than the Father. It shows the willingness of the three to have the Father receive the glory from all. It is the function of the Father to receive all the glory contained in the full Trinity. We can obviously see that the Son's perfect reflection of the Father's glory makes them equal. However, the Father does have the superior role as seen in the reigning from heaven passages.

Hebrews 1, John 1, and Genesis 1 all tell of the creation of the world. They all show that creation was a well-planned, choreographed design. The grand architect, the Father, purposefully designed His creation to glorify Himself. Christ even tells His creation that the Father is to be glorified.[178] People often do not want to give the Father the glory He deserves. Time and again over the centuries, man has tried to give the glory to the Son, and in recent days, many denominations have tried to give all glory to the Holy Spirit, feeling He has been left out. As a collective, the Son and the Holy Spirit give the glory back to the Father.

In Romans 1, we see that people often give the rightful glory of God and place it on something created. They have created their own gods and their own concepts of how life began to take root. Through time, we see cultural groups like Hindus create multiple gods to substitute for the real God. In the modern era, we have seen everything from ancient aliens to spontaneous combustion of matter as

---

178 Mt. 5:16.

explanations of how the world was created.[179] However, they all have one thing in common: they believe something is eternal. They cannot explain how the matter came about, so they have to believe it is eternal. If it is spontaneous, there still has to be matter to have a reaction. Paul Davies writes, "Trying to make life by mixing chemicals in a test tube is like soldering switches and wires in an attempt to produce Windows 98. It won't work because it addresses the problem at the wrong conceptual level."[180] The Father, as the grand architect, is the eternal and all-powerful being that has a mind and will to make the universe exist. All other religions and worldviews come short of what the Trinity provides as a logical explanation of creation.

It can only be a God that has fellowship outside of time that can produce a people that too is in fellowship with each other and with the creator. For a creation theory to work, it also has to have an ultimate single being that has always been with the power to create. No one can create something better than themselves. When it comes to our origins, there must be an understanding that something started the process of life. The Father, as the grand architect, is the Supreme Being outside of creation and time that is and became the designer of life. Darwin believed in the survival of the fittest and that life would get better with each generation. However, his view of beginnings starts with the eternal being matter, and from there it all gets better. As Davies has said, this is addressing the problem from the wrong conceptual level. There is no logical explanation why only people can communicate and all other parts of creation cannot. Creationists state that all mankind is made in the image of God, and it is through the Father's design that we are created to think, communicate, and

---

179 Ancient Aliens History channel tv show
180 Paul Davies, "The Secret of Life Won't be Cooked Up in a Chemistry Lab." (Guardian: January 13, 2013), 1.

create.[181] He tells us this was His plan from the start. Thomas Nagel and others, who associate with Darwin, do not want to see common sense reasoning as an option because it simply goes against their desire to have an existence of God. They simply want to point out that they do not know and they have no satisfying answers.[182]

The Father is not only the architect, but He is the person who shares with us the proper relationship a father is to have with his children. He has called Himself Father to denote a correct definition of His role. It is through the ultimate Father that all other uses of father are judged. God demonstrates to His people the proper function of a human father to his children. He showed us how by living His personal relationship with mankind. He demonstrated to Moses that He is holy and approaching Him incorrectly was dangerous.[183] He talked with Moses and reasoned with Him so that God's name would be preserved even when the people all deserved destruction.[184] The Father also gave Moses the Ten Commandments to follow as a guide for life.[185]

After the creation account, God tells Adam that he is to multiply and have children.[186] With this command, Adam and Eve procreated and had Cain.[187] Now He is to teach His creation how to be a father. One of the first things a father is to do is provide for his sons.

Provisions for life can be broken down into several general categories: food, water, shelter, and clothing. Noting that the clothing need came after the fall of man. God did not go into great detail as to how lavish the provisions were to be, so it will be assumed that the

---

181Gn. 1:26.
182 Pearcey, 230-231.
183 Ex 3
184 Ex 32:11-14
185 Ex 20
186 Gn. 1:28.
187 Gn. 4:1

father should provide for his family as he would provide things for himself.[188] As a part of that provision, the father is to provide protection to his daughters.[189] It should be noted that the provisions that are to be provided have an expiration date. Each child is expected to learn a trade and leave the home at the completion of training[190]. Genesis 2:24 also sets a separation date at the wedding ceremony. Once the child is old enough to work and provide for themselves, they are to marry, and all the provisions of the father are with the new family. The requirement has been paid, and the couple is to provide for themselves. The attachment to the family is cut. Giving to the child after the wedding is not prohibited unless it makes them reliant on the father for their provisions. A father and mother are to help make this possible and not hinder the new relationship.

All able men and women were to leave when they were ready to work. The childhood years were to be a time of planning and instruction.[191] When they reached their twelfth birthday, they were to be ready for paid work, and by the time they were in their late teens, they were expected to be working and preparing for marriage. The son would enter manhood at the age of twelve. He would be counted as one of the ten men needed for a synagogue to be built in the home city.[192] This would also start the father's negotiations with the potential bride's father concerning whom his son would marry.[193] It is during these short years that the father shows his provision for his child.[194]

---

188 Mt. 7:11.
189 Ex. 30:4
190 Ralph Gower, Mannors and Customs Bible Times, (Chicago: Moody, 2005), 60.
191 Pr. 1:8.
192 Gower, 60.
193 Gower, 60-61.
194 Gn. 2:24.

The Father shows us that He had planned the birth of His Son in Luke 2. It also shares that He grew in His Father's favor as he grew up to be a man.[195] When he reached the age of twelve, Jesus was pleasing His Father and went about doing His Father's business.[196] The Father was proud of His son and took care of His needs. [197]

The father was also to bless his children. From the Old Testament, it was very common for the oldest son to be blessed, and on occasion, a second blessing was given to other children.[198] The oldest son was the one to take the father's place of authority when he passed. On many occasions, wise words or special instructions were given to a child who has been given this special moment. In the blessing, there are always a few components that do not change. The first is that there must be one in greater authority giving the blessing to the one with less authority. It is to be a very special time where specific instructions or pronouncements are to be given. It is a time of celebration, and many times it is followed up with the foreseen death of the family leader.[199] In the case of David in 1 Kings, we also have a national leader ready to pronounce who the new leader was to be, so the people knew the king's wishes.

In the New Testament, we have 2 Timothy as a letter from the imprisoned Paul to his son in the ministry, Timothy. The entire book shows how Paul is giving his one last instruction to the young church

---

195 Lk. 2:52.

196 Lk. 2:49.

197 Lk. 2:22.

198 Gen 27:27-29; 2: 38-40; Gen 48:15-16; 1 Kings 2:1-4.

199 William E Brown, "Blessing" Baker's Evangelical Dictionary of the Bible, http://www.biblestudy tools.com/dictionaries/bakers-evangelical-dictionary/blessing.html (accessed August 15, 2016).

leader to be, and he does it in an open letter to the church to ensure that the church will accept this new leader.[200]

John 21:15-22 is Jesus' last words to Peter. It is one last conversation of instruction and blessing on Peter. He will have the Spirit of God in his life, and he will live like Jesus, not by his own power, but by the power of the Holy Spirit. This same Spirit was descending like a dove onto Jesus from the Father at His baptism.[201] The Father, in front of others, is showing that Jesus truly is God sent by God and has the Spirit of God. The people are to listen to His instructions. Jesus is the gift of salvation from the Father.

The Father is the one giving the blessing to the Son. The Christian father should take a special, well-planned coming-of-age blessing for his children based on how the Father interacted with Jesus. There is no longer a need to pass off the blessing at the end of life. The fluid society that we live in today more closely matches the provider role than the Old Testament blessing role of waiting until the father thinks death is close. The book *Wild Things: The Art of Nurturing Boys* gives fathers many ideas on how to have a special blessing ceremony. Some men need to write their words out, and others want to be off the cuff. Whichever way is best for the father does not matter; it is the message that matters. Fathers will need to not follow modern customs alone for this blessing. They will want to follow the outline that the Father has for Jesus laid out in scripture. The book encourages us to follow the example of our heavenly Father and bless our sons for a special life mission of service to His work. When planning this rite of passage remember these tips: stroke the wildness of his heart; keep his stories alive; don't use the cookie-cutter; nothing is more stressful and scarier for a boy than having the world revolve around him; involve older men; open some windows for him; give him a gift; affirm with words;

---

200 John Polhill, Paul and His Letters, (Nashville: B&H Academic, 1999), 428.
201 Lk. 3:21-22.

let the words of others be a mystery. If you need to let the women be a part, make their part a separate place and time.[202] If Fathers search the heavenly Father for the ability to interact and communicate, then God will be better known, and His instructions will be of great service.

The largest section of scriptures that God gives his people is that the Father is the giver of laws. He does not give laws to hurt us, but that we might have a greater life. The two verses that all parents know are Ephesians 6:1 and Exodus 20:12. Children, obey your parents and honor your father and mother. The two have the same promise of a long life. Both the New and Old Testaments have this as a primary focus for the children being raised for the Father. The Father sees this one command as so important that He places a promise to go with it. He has promised a long life to those who obey. Adam and Eve, the first children in the garden, broke God's command to obey, and the punishment was severe. The opposite of the blessing in the previous paragraphs is a curse. Adam and Eve were the ones to disobey and not honor the Father, so instead of being blessed, the creation was cursed.[203]

A large part of obedience is knowing the rules and regulations. The Son knows just how important this is to the Father because He stated in Matthew 28:20 that all the commands I give to you today are to be known and obeyed. The fathers are to share with their sons a proper relationship with boundaries. The book of Proverbs is primarily a letter from Solomon to his son on the proper way to live. "Listen, my son, to your father's instruction, and do not reject your mother's teaching.[204] Then the writers continuously instruct their children in the ways of wisdom and the folly of not listening. Man

---

202 Stephen James and David Thomas, Wild Things: The Art of Nurturing Boys, (Carol Stream, IL: Tyndale, 2009), 288-291.
203 Gn. 3.
204 Pr. 1:8 (HCSB).

must build a relationship with their children if he wishes to follow in our heavenly Father's path. It is easy for the father to see the folly of not obeying because he has been there, yet many fathers do not want to listen to their Father's instruction, even when they know He knows everything. He can see the past and the future, yet it is hard for them to be guided by his wisdom.

The Father was constantly sharing with his Son how to live, and the Son would come to His Father again and again.[205] On one occasion, Jesus is telling the people that unless the Father sends them to me, I will do nothing.[206] Jesus clearly is the one who comes to save the lost, but from this verse, it is the Father who places the lost in the hands of Jesus. The Father knows, and the Son listens. Obedience to the Father and His laws is crucial to a good relationship with Him, and hence our relationship to the Son who came to save us from our sins.

God shows Himself as a father, not because He is more for men than women. He loves all people equally. He set up the father figure to represent what fatherhood was. The person of the Father shows himself throughout the Old Testament as a loving God who specially created people. He made them in his very image and desires for us to be like Him.[207] Even when Adam sinned, He did not wish to give up on His children but instead provided a way for them to come back into a relationship with Him.

The New Testament shows us many of His desires to be personable with His creation. The Father desires a relationship with people, and He provided that opportunity through the Son to show that relationship. All of those who partake of the Son must have a relationship with the Father. Therefore, all others cannot call Him

---

205 Pr. 1:10; 2:1-8; 3:1-3; 4:1-6; 5:1-5; 6:1-5; 8:32-36; 13:1-4.
206Jn. 6:43.
207 Gn. 1:26.

Father, and He will not acknowledge them as His. Those who call Him Father will be blessed with good gifts to help further His kingdom.[208] One such gift is the ability to speak to others so they, too, can have a relationship with the Father. He will help us with our words in prayer and proclamation by directing the Spirit to give the Christian the words to say.[209] Matthew 11:28 admonishes us to take our work and rest from the Father. He is here to come alongside us and help us with our burdens. Just as the Father is here taking care of the overburdened load humanity possesses, He wants His children to be just as merciful to those around them as he was to them.[210] As with all relationships, there must be love, and it has to come from both parties. In John 8:42-47, it shows three parties showing love to the other. To have God as a Father, you must love the Son. The Son loved the Father and was sent by Him. The one who listens and does the work of the Son knows the Father and is loved by Him. Even in distinguishing the Father, the Son is in sync and harmony with the entire plan.

Our relationship must have a two-way conversation that involves both the Father and the Son. To properly communicate, there must be an understanding of who the other person is and how they reciprocate their communication. Man must realize the Father is perfect and so is His residence, heaven. Sinners cannot be in His presence with the guilt of sin, and we fall short of God's glory.[211] However, the Son demonstrated his own love for us even while we were still in the muck of sin; he was willing to die for us.[212] Our sin becomes so difficult that there are times when God expresses His remorse for creating something that will turn completely away from Him.[213] He was still

---

208 Mt. 7:11.
209 Mt.. 10:20.
210 Lk. 6:36.
211 Rm. 3:23.
212 Rm. 5:8.
213 Gn. 6:5-6.

not willing to give up on His people. He was willing to give us laws to follow and obey.[214] He desired for us to have His identity, and He constantly provides for us just as a father should. [215] He is always there, and He has provided a way for people to have a Father-child relationship. This is often a stark contrast to the relationships we have and experience with others, but He is the ultimate example. There have been many times throughout history that fathers have been absent from the family, and each time, the family has suffered due to this loss. God has provided the perfect relationship before His creation, but the people must understand who He is before they can partake.

The Father is holy, and so is His name. Matthew 6:9 and John 14:6 start with the opening of Jesus' prayer. This is an example for Jesus's disciples. These verses tell us to whom we should pray, and also tell us about His characteristics. He is there as our Father. Our adoption through the Son allows us to go straight to the Father with our petitions and praise. He is high and lifted up and worthy to be praised.[216] His location is the throne room of heaven, where only the holiest and majestic God can be seated.[217]

"Your name be honored as holy."[218] This means that not only is God holy, but so is His name. Ken Hemphill's father sums up this verse when he told his son, "I have only one piece of advice to give you. I want to remind you that you bear my name. . . . The name "Hemphill" stands for something. So don't take my name anywhere I wouldn't take it, and don't involve my name in anything I wouldn't

---

214 Dt. 5:4-21.
215 Rm. 8:15.
216 Jn. 1:23.
217 Is. 6:3-5.
218 Mt. 6:9.

do."[219] The adopted Christian should be even more mindful of how they treat the holy name of the Father. The privilege to speak to the Father as we are able, cost His Son His life. Now there is a generation of children that might lose this understanding of God. This concept is hard to teach because many do not have a father figure in the home, and many of the ones that still have a father at home are not living out the example they should. However, the Father of all creation has given Himself to us and is willing to be the example we all long to see. Without the Father, we have no relationship to base all other relationships. Christianity is the only religion with an intimate God who is all-powerful. The person of the Father and understanding of His role are essential in how one lives. Many will say that they have not thought about it, and how will that affect life? It is not a question of making a philosophical argument; it is a part of our lives as a presumed reality until one comes to a place where they wrestle with this concept of a God willing to be an example, Father.

Just two generations ago, it was very common in America that a family would expect there to be a father in the home. In just a few years, we have 40 percent of American children sleeping in the same house as their father.[220] American men have relinquished their role of father, and American women have helped this decline as well. Not having a father in the home has greatly reduced the influence that a father has on his children. The further the country strays from God the Father's perfect example, the more people reject the role of father altogether. "The result is a tremendous loss of self. So acute is this brokenness that men have become incredibly adept at diverting our focus from what is missing."[221] The children are missing their

---

219 Ken Hemphill, The Prayer of Jesus, (Nashville: Broadman and Holman, 2001), 48.
220 David Blankenhorn, Fatherless America. (New York: Basic Books, 1995), 1.
221 Eric Mason, Manhood Restored. (Nashville: B&H Publishing Group, 2013), 22.

relationship with God even more than their father. They will find an alternative if they lose their earthly or heavenly father, but no substitute will be satisfactory.

How do fathers keep them close? This is done by going to the Father and following His instructions. Often, one stops at Colossians 3:20 and forgets the next verse. Fathers do not exasperate your children, so they won't become discouraged.[222] The word, for exasperate can mean provoke, embitter, or irritate. Fathers are to show discipline to their children, but they are to understand they are loved and there is a reason for discipline to take place.[223] This is why the Father gives us the law. Yes, the law is here to help us, not to save us from our problems.[224] Discipline shows everyone that they have transgressed the law, but the Father wants to show His children that we are loved even in discipline.[225] This is why He was willing to send His Son to take the problems of Sin and have them fully punished.

It tells us in Luke 15:8 that the Father desires a relationship with His people and wishes for us to come clean with our sin because He sees even our most hidden secrets.[226] The Father already knows all, and He is willing to forgive just as we are forgiving others.[227] Not only does the Father want to forgive and have us confess our sins to Him, but He also wants us to be proud of Him. The sacrifice of His Son is the price to be paid. The Son said that I will proclaim you before my Father if and only if you confess me before other men.[228] Jesus said

---

222 Col. 3:21.
223 Reid Patton, "Father's Do Not Embitter Your Children", Journey on Today. June 29, 2016. http://brentwoodbaptist.com/journeyon-today/2016-06-29/ (accessed March 14, 2017).
224 1 Ch. 22:12.
225 Heb. 12:6.
226 Mt. 6:4.
227 Mt. 6:14.
228 Mt. 10:32.

you get to pray and have your sins forgiven only through Me. The relationship with the Father is predicated on the relationship with the Son.

"No other human explained God the Father more effectively than Jesus. God's fatherhood of us is rooted in God's fatherhood of Jesus. Jesus' entire earthly ministry was driven by His understanding of and His relationship with God as His Father.[229] The Son has been in eternal fellowship with the Father."[230]

The Father is the great architect of the universe, recipient of all Glory, the superior person in the Trinity, demonstrator of proper relationships to His people, and the great provider. He also takes pleasure in His Son, blesses the next generation, gives the laws, shows His holiness, and is the adopter of His chosen people. The person of the Father is distinct from the other persons of the Trinity, but as stated before, you cannot separate, but you can distinguish their personhood.

---

229 Jn. 1:18.
230 Mason, p. 33

CHAPTER 11
The Son as Person

T he desire to study the person of Jesus in relationship with the Trinity is quite overwhelming. This is due in part because of the dual nature of the Son. He is both man and God. Many books have been written focusing on His deity. Fewer books focus on His humanity and His relation to man. In the biblical text, He is often referred to as the Son of man. In many cases, this is the defining term He gives Himself. The distinguishing characteristics of the person of Jesus that set Him apart from the two other persons, will be the goal of this section. It has been identified that they are the same essence in section one. Now the discussion of the Son, Jesus, turns to His person within the Trinity and the distinction, not the separation of character.

The gospel of John will be used as the guide for this study because John shows a great desire to help his readers understand the Son and His purpose. The gospel of John was written for those who were not in Christ so they could see through his words all that Jesus had done, and to prove that Jesus is God. After looking at the last chapter of John, he was concerned with the reader seeing the signs of Jesus being God and convincing the reader that Jesus is worth following. The Son came to Earth in human flesh and was both man and God.[231] [232] This first distinction is the most obvious. The Son is the only person of the

---

231 Frank W. Scott, The Preacher's Complete Homiletic Commentary: On the Gospel According to John, (Grand Rapids: Baker Books, 1996.), 10.
232Jn. 1:14; 17:11; 17:18; 19:7; 21:24-25

Trinity to be a man. He was the only one born a man, to die as a man, and to be raised back to life. The other two have always been spirits alone. This concept is so difficult to understand that even modern books like *The Shack* treat all the persons of the Trinity as dying for man on the cross.

"While the literary device of an unconventional "trinity" of divine persons is itself sub-biblical and dangerous, the theological explanations are worse. "Papa," tells Mack of the time when the three persons of the Trinity "spoke ourselves into human existence as the Son of God." Nowhere in the Bible is the Father or the Spirit described as taking on human existence. The Christology of the book is likewise confused. "Papa," tells Mack that, though Jesus is fully God, "he has *never* drawn upon his nature as God to do anything. He has only lived out of his relationship with me, living in the very same manner that I desire to be in a relationship with every human being." When Jesus healed the blind, "He did so only as a dependent, limited human being trusting in my life and power to be at work within him and through him. Jesus, as a human being, had no power within himself to heal anyone."[233]

This is clearly modalism heresy from a previous chapter, and great care should be given to our understanding of the Son.

Looking at the gospel in chapter one, the Son has been and is at the center of the universe.[234] The beginning of John starts with the fact that the Word "was." [235] He never came into being but was already at creation. It was not His birth to Mary that started the distinction of the Father and the Son. It never says that He was created; hence, He was

---

233 Mohler, R. Albert, "The Shack-The Missing Art of Evangelical Discernment" R. Albert Mohler Blog. www.albertmohler.com/2010/01/27the-shack-the-missing-art-of-evangelical-discernment, (Accessed March 29, 2017).
234 Scott, 13.
235 Jn. 1:1.

before the creation of anything.[236] The Word was with God, and the Word was God. This simple phrase tells us that there are two persons being represented, and they are both equal in deity.[237] It also shows that Jesus, the Son, was both with the Father and apart from the Father at the same time. The word use is very distinctive as it reads both "with" and "was" in the same phrase.

The Word was to be seen as one in essence with the Father and yet a different person. The two are together in all of their responsibilities, but they play different roles in accomplishing the tasks. God the Father has the plans; God the Son makes the creation plan happen. In the creation, the Father was the architect, and Jesus was the builder. Genesis also tells us there will be a third person at work in the creation.[238] He will be discussed in the next chapter; however, the overseeing work of creation is found in the person of the Holy Spirit.

This Word was not only the creator of all things, but He became flesh and dwelt among us.[239] Not only did God make us with an intricate plan, but He had plans from the beginning to come and live with His creation after they sinned and deserved punishment. Genesis 1:31 tells of the great plans that had been made complete, and God said it was very good. There was fellowship between God and man, and Genesis 3:8 demonstrates that the break of fellowship was quite obvious. The Father had been separated from His creation, and in order for this schism to be fixed, there had to be remuneration for the guilt of sin now on the created man. Bruce Ware, in his book, *The Man Christ Jesus,* tells in simple terms why Jesus must be both man and God. If God were to create another Adam and he was able to live

---

236 Jn. 1:3.
237 Merril Tenney, The Expositor's Bible Commentary vol. 9. (Grand Rapids: Zondervan, 1981), 28.
238 Ware, 51.
239 Jn. 1:14; 7:11: 7:18.

a sinless life, and if he was willing to die for the sins of humanity, would it be sufficient? The answer is no. He might be able to take the initial punishment of the sin in death, but he could not say, "It is finished." Only God would be able to take the full punishment of Sin and satisfy the wrath of the Father in full punishment.[240] The Father was willing to send the Son, and the Son was submissive to the Father. He did not only come for those in Israel, but for the scattered as well.[241]

Genesis 1:3, God spoke, and there was light. Day one's creation masterpiece is the same as the light in John 1:5. Here, the passage relates that the light of the world must come to the people, and the true light was to be the Son. The light and life of the Son would be all a person would need for salvation.[242] The Father has sent the Son into the world so that we might see His holiness and have our ransom of sin paid by the only one worthy to pay the price, Jesus Christ, the Son of God. "Long ago God spoke to the fathers by the prophets at different times and in different ways. In these last days, He has spoken to us by His Son. God has appointed Him heir of all things and made the universe through Him. The Son is the radiance of God's glory and the exact expression of His nature, sustaining all things by His powerful word. After making purification for our sins, He sat down at the right hand of the Majesty on high.[243] The Son was the person who created all that exists, and He is the one who will take upon Himself the flesh of men and dwell among His people. Jesus would not come as a man like Adam but would live as a man who was both truly God and truly man.[244] "He will be great, and He will be called the Son of the Most-High, and the Lord God will give Him the throne of His

240 Bruce A. Ware, The Man Christ Jesus. (Wheaton: Crossway, 2013), 111-112.
241 Jn. 11:50-52
242 Jn. 1:4-5; 5:25; 8:12; 9:5; 12:35-36, 12:46.
243 Heb. 1:1-4 (HCSB)."
244 Begg, 101.

father David[245]." This begs the question of how Jesus could be God and man at the same time. The nature of the Kenosis or self-emptying denotes that Christ left nothing of his deity out, but rather put all of his deity into His humanity. It is a form of math where we see addition and subtraction, but God sees one person, the Son of God, and the Son of man are one.[246] Another place to help understand the oneness of Jesus both in divinity and humanity is in John 1. John shows that the Word was both with God and the Word was God. It is hard for us to comprehend that Jesus was both with God and was God at the same time, saying there has always been one God.[247] It tells us in John 1:14 that this same singular God comes to earth in the flesh as man to dwell among the people. "Make your own attitude that of Christ Jesus, who, existing in the form of God, did not consider equality with God as something to be used for His own advantage. Instead, He emptied Himself by assuming the form of a slave, taking on the likeness of men. And when He had come as a man in His external form, He humbled Himself by becoming obedient to the point of death - even death on a cross.[248]" He was poured out completely into Jesus. This action of the Son shows just how serious His love for His creation would take form. Jesus had a plan, and that plan was to redeem humanity back to the Father.[249]

Jesus shows us the care and love of the Trinity through His actions. He is willing to go without food and water for forty days in the wilderness.[250] He was obedient to the Holy Spirit in being taken, and He was showing all humanity that there is nothing He has not gone through and still has no sin. He was also hit with a mighty onslaught

---

245 Lk. 1:32 (HCSB)
246 Ware, The Man Christ Jesus, 18-20.
247 Jn. 1:1.
248 Phi. 2:5-8 (HCSB)
249 Jn. 3:31-36.
250 Mk. 1:12-13.

of demons that invaded the land upon His arrival.[251] He was able to show His compassion by casting many out. In addition to the many miracles, Jesus shows us that the Son has feelings of sadness and anger, just as all humanity feels for others who are close. John 11:35 and 11:38 tell of the death of a close friend, Lazarus. Just before his own death would soon come, Jesus realizes that the time had not come for him to visit because Lazarus was still alive. He was willing to be led by the Spirit in a submissive posture, knowing that the Father had a plan for a future date.[252] Jesus waited two extra days so that the Father would get the glory. This delay was for an even greater miracle to take place, but Jesus is recorded as one who was weeping and being angry, even though he knew the end results.[253]

The Son's entrance to earth was to eradicate the sin problem of those who accepted His sacrifice for their sin. To do this, the Son came as a baby to a simple, poor family and not as a full-grown man with great pomp and circumstance. Luke 1:35 is the start of the story of how a young, poor woman, not yet married, was told she would have a child, and He would be the Son of God. Her response in verse forty-three shows just how unbelievable it would be for some people to accept this great news. The creator of the universe humbled himself to the poor of Israel. Then, as He "grew, he increased in wisdom and in stature and in favor with God and man."[254] At the time of His ministry, Jesus showed people over and over that He was the Son of God who had come to live His life at the will of the Father with the

---

251 Begg, 27-28.
252 Jn. 11:6-7.
253 Jn. 11:33-35.
254 Lk. 2:52

power of the Spirit.[255] He lived a full and sinless life[256] so that mankind would have a perfect sacrifice for the Father.

There were several instances where it is made clear that Jesus was set apart for His special ministry. This anointing is what gives Him the ability to be called the Christ or the Messiah. The Messiah is "the one promised of God as the great deliverer, and who was to be in a preeminent and altogether unique sense the anointed, or the Messiah, of God. . . . It became known as the coming of the King."[257] He was called the Messiah, and the Greek word equivalent is "Christ."[258] The people put upon the definition what they wanted to hear and wanted, an earthly king to take away all their problems.

The Son who came as the Christ also came as the King of Kings. Even from the start, He knew who He was and did not correct Nathanael when he cried out, "You are the Son of God! You are the King of Israel![259]" However, Jesus tells Pilate that His kingdom is real, it just doesn't happen to be on the corrupt earth.[260] Pilate gave Him the title anyway when he placed it on the cross.[261] The title was given to Him despite the strong objections of the Jewish leaders.

The ordinance of baptism and the Trinitarian work of the Father sending of the Son with the ever-present Spirit guiding His steps set forth how the Christian is to live. The ordinance of the Lord's Supper is unique to the Son.[262] Here, the passage is directed to the full plan of the Father carried out by the Son. "Take and eat it, this is my body."

---

255 Jn. 1:1; 3:16; 5:35-40; 5:46-47.
256 1 Pt. 2:22-24.
257 Unger, 839.
258 Jn 1:41; 4:26; 5:25; 11:27
259 Jn. 1:49 (HCSB)
260 Jn. 18:36-37.
261 Jn. 19:19.
262 Lk. 22:19, Mk. 14:22-26, Mt. 26:26-30.

There are countless books on the Lord's Supper and its meanings, but all four mainline views agree that Jesus is the Son and He is central in the Lord's Supper.[263] When Jesus says, "This is my body." He is telling His disciples that until He returns to the earth, remember the things I have taught you from the moment of my arrival until the going up again. You are to remember and put into practice all that I have taught.[264] The Son was to be a sacrifice for the sins of all who accept His gift of salvation, but His life teachings were to be remembered and kept. The Son was sent to show man how he could relate to the Father. Jesus was sent to be an example and in so doing proved Himself to be God over and over again.

There have been many descriptions of the Son through the New Testament. Each one tells us a little more about the man and His characteristics. Two primary examples are the description of being the light and the life of the world. The Son is the one to bring the message of the Father's truth to the people. Anyone who hears the Son and believes the Father will have eternal life.[265] The Son and the Father play a role in salvation, but the Son is the one who directly delivers the message. John 5:30 states it is easy to see that the Son is the just judge. Not because He is the Son, but because the Son listens to the Father. This submissive role is stated over thirty times in John, and this submission should be seen in all relationships.[266] No matter the relationship, Jesus is showing us that an equal role can still be submissive and proper if the example of the Son is taken. Jesus always takes the glory from His people and gives it to the Father. It is due to His example and actions that eternal life is brought to people through His sacrifice on the cross for the salvation of the people. All who

---

263 Thomas Schreiner, and Matthew Crawford, The Lord's Supper, (Nashville: B&H Printing, 2010), 6.
264 Mt. 28:20.
265 Jn. 5:24.
266 Ware, Father, Son, Holy Spirit, .77.

follow the light of Jesus will be saved.[267] Again, Jesus states that He is the light, and by this light, salvation is possible. His position of judgment comes from both the Father and the Son.[268] The Trinity is still one in essence and will always work as a unit, even if we differentiate the persons. The Son was sent so that people could see who He was and thereby know the Father and experience His salvation.[269]

Jesus has many names that He is called while on earth. "Seed of the Woman, the True Prophet, Great High Priest, Conquering King, Suffering Servant, and Lamb on the Throne" are just a few of the names that are fulfilled in Jesus.[270] Many of these will not be mentioned here due to the limited scope of the book of John. The Son has played a very special role for His people. He is the Living Water.[271] Without eternal water, we cannot have eternal life. Once we have the water of salvation, we must understand that He is the one providing the water and the one who is keeping His sheep. Any other way that one tries to gain eternal security is a thief, and the Son will cast him out. He will keep all the people that the Father gives Him, and none of these will be lost.[272]

A Trinity that created all and made it very good is the same God that demands that His creation be perfect if they are to enter His presence at death. The death of man came because of sin; therefore, people are fully reliant on the Son for eternal life. No sin can enter heaven because God is Holy, Isaiah 6; it declares that Isaiah became undone at the thought of seeing God and not being worthy. Isaiah was

---

267 Jn. 8:12-13; 12:46.
268 Jn. 8:16.
269 Jn. 9:5; 12:36
270 Begg, .9.
271 Jn. 4:10; 8:50.
272 Jn. 10:1-8.

expecting death to happen at any moment because he was very aware of his sin problem. Moses was given the law and the sacrificial system, not to be perfect, but that the promise of a perfect sacrifice might one day come. This type of sign was waiting for the antitype. When Christ comes to the earth, He is declaring, "I am the Lamb of God."[273] I have come to be that sacrifice. I am able to take away the sins of the world, and mankind can come to the Father through me.

The power of the name of Jesus was used to do many miraculous things. All authority in heaven and earth resided in the name of Jesus.[274] It is clear that the name of "Jesus" is to be used when the Christian prays. John 16:23-24 is just before the arrest of Jesus. It is the admonishment to the new followers that there will be a time when Jesus will not walk with His friends on the earth as He once did. They will need to know that they are not being left to die with no help. It does seem that the disciples of Jesus have not yet fully understood that Jesus will soon die on the cross. This conversation will come to be central in their physical survival, and the gospel being spread will be accomplished only in the power of Jesus. He is giving the disciples, through prayer, an understanding of how to live life from that time forward. Jesus is telling them to pray to the Father just as I have been showing you and ask Him all that you would ask Me. Use my name, and you will receive all with abundant joy. They will need to quickly understand that the Matthew 6:10 passage must first be understood in this context. They will always have to keep the Father's will first, and when they ask, all will be freely given, and great joy will abound. Man is to pray to the Father, in the name of the Son and in the power of the Spirit.

---

273 Jn. 1:29.
274 Mt. 28:19-20.

In the last chapter of John, John stated, "And there are also many other things that Jesus did, which, if they were written one by one, I suppose not even the world itself could contain the books that would be written."[275] It is through the conclusion of John that the humanity of Jesus has such a breadth of teaching and understanding that no matter the size of the book written, you would just be scratching the surface of His person.

---

275 Jn. 21:25.

CHAPTER 12
The Person of the Holy Spirit

There are multiple transitions of focus recognized between the persons of the Trinity. Each person works together on their individual tasks throughout the Bible, but there seems to be a primary person leading the people at any given time. John 16:5-17 shows us the transition from the Father to the Son. The Father is the one who sends Jesus to accomplish the task of salvation for mankind. Then the Son, after accomplishing His human task, sends the Holy Spirit. As Jesus is preparing for this transition, He introduces the Holy Spirit to His disciples, even though the disciples should already be familiar with the Spirit, having studied His works in the Psalms. They will be taking the next step in living without Jesus by their side, and they need to understand the third person of the Trinity and His relationship to them. As a last parting word to the whole group, "He [Jesus] spoke to them again and said, "Peace be with you. As the Father has sent me, so I send you." Then He breathed on them and said to them, "Receive the Holy Spirit."[276]

The last-mentioned person of the Trinity, in distinction within the Trinity, is the Holy Spirit. Although the Father may have the least understanding of how His role fits, the Holy Spirit has "Spirit" in His name. This makes it very difficult for many to explain the personhood of the Spirit if they only comprehend relationships that are exclusive to human-to-human interaction. To make matters a little harder, the

---

276 Jn. 21:21-22 (NLT)

Holy Spirit in the Greek uses a neuter noun. The neuter form has the English reader say "it" instead of "him" for the masculine form or "her" for the feminine form. Jesus puts this to rest in John 16:13-14. Here, Jesus uses the masculine pronoun □□□□□□□□ekeiuos to speak of the Holy Spirit. The reader would expect a neuter pronoun with a normal neuter usage, but Jesus wanted it made clear that the Holy Spirit was indeed a masculine person with the use of "He". It is noted by many scholars that the Holy Spirit is indeed a person and not an impersonal force.[277] Another example comes from John 15:26. For a being to be a person, there must be personal qualities. In the coming section, each personal characteristic will be closely examined, and the role that the Spirit plays will be examined in relation to one of the persons of the Trinity.

The personhood of the Holy Spirit can be very challenging. The "Spirit is said to be a teacher, comforter, and guide. When we sin against or grieve Him, it is an action against a person. The Spirit also searches, selects, and reveals things to people."[278] It is possible to lie to the Spirit, and it turns out that this was a very bad idea. It was such a bad idea that two people died instantly when this sin was committed and affirmed by the early church.[279] Next to lying to the Holy Spirit is blaspheming the Holy Spirit. Jesus tells the crowd that this sin is unforgivable.[280] Only slightly less is the sin of grieving and quenching of the Holy Spirit.[281] "The Holy Spirit is a person, not a force, and that person is God."[282] The Christian must be careful in all his actions concerning the Spirit. All the actions must go through the filter of the

---

277 Erickson, 784.
278 R.C. Sproul, The Mystery of the Holy Spirit. Ross Shire, Scotland: Christian Focus 2011), 16-17.
279 Acts 5:3-4.
280 Mt. 12:31 and Mk. 3:29.
281 Eph. 4:30, 1 Th. 5:19.
282 Erickson, 786.

Spirit. Not being one with the Spirit will lead to suppression of our best actions and fall into the category of grieving or quenching the Spirit, making it possible to serve God. Obedience to the Bible and the Holy Spirit's commands is what allows us to worship. Without obedience, there is no real worship.

Now that it has been established that the Spirit is a person, we must not confuse the thought that He is human. He, like the Father, is not and never will be human. This does not mean He is not a person. Personality is defined as: "In theology as in metaphysics, personality is that which constitutes a person. Says Locke: 'A person is a thinking intelligent being that has reason and reflection, and can consider itself as itself, the same thinking thing in different times and places.' In other words, the distinguishing marks of personality are self-consciousness and freedom."[283] It is in the spirit of the man that makes a man a person with choices and decisions, not the flesh. He is described quite vividly in John 3:8 as one "like the wind." The term for wind is also where we get the word for breath. This is the life-giving person of God. When God breathed life into the first man, Adam, it was the Holy Spirit doing the breathing. This was a unique creation in that no other creation had the Spirit breathing life. All the others were spoken into existence by the Son. Genesis 2:1-7 tells us first, The Son spoke all the needed parts into existence. Second, the Father formed the man out of the dust of the ground. The third and final act was the Holy Spirit breathing life into his nose. In 1 Corinthians 2:9-16, the mind of Christ and the will of the Father are only able to be seen by men through the Spirit. It is the Spirit that can penetrate like the wind and can know all that needs to be known. Just as the wind cannot be seen, but the effects are evident, so is the power of the Spirit alive and working in humanity. This is why Jesus alludes to the wind in John 3. "We are not by nature spiritual persons. A

---

283 Unger, "personality"

Person cannot discern spiritual things until that person is first made alive to spiritual things by the Spirit of God. It is the Spirit's work of regeneration, of spiritual rebirth, that enables us to have spiritual discernment."[284] All humanity was made in the image of God[285] and are persons, but not all will have the needed spiritual rebirth of the Spirit to obtain eternal life without the work of the Spirit.[286]

The Holy Spirit is not only active in the generation of man and sustaining life, but He also regenerated man's spirit after sin destroyed the relationship with man and God. It is only through His power of regeneration that man can obtain this new relationship. At the beginning of the New Testament, the Holy Spirit is seen in a more active role with individuals than in the Old Testament, but His creation of individuals is a big part of what sets apart His person. "What God creates, He also sustains, upholding all things by His power.[287] He also has interacted with individual people to perform the power of God through His acts. The usage of the "Spirit of God" can be seen in Acts 2:16-21. Peter is letting the people know that the power of the Spirit is the same as the power of God, and the two should be seen as interchangeable.[288] However, the Spirit's responsibility in the Old Testament does seem to greatly change as the Son comes, and it will change again when the Son departs; however, there is not one part of the Holy Spirit that changes in His being.

Looking at the Old Testament first, the Spirit has the responsibility of coming to a group of people and abiding with them as long as the covenant is being kept. The Lord your God will go before you and

---

284 Sproul, The Mystery of the Holy Spirit., 14
285 Gn. 1:27.
286 Jn. 3:16
287 Ibid, 71
288 Erickson, 790.

drive out those who did not listen.[289] He also stated that if you, the promised people, fall away from my covenant, I will destroy you as well.[290] It is the power of the Holy Spirit that the people would see going before them in battle. It is also in the Spirit that God gave abilities to the people to serve Him in the Old Testament. In the book of Numbers, Bezalel was given the special gifts of crafting the temple for worship. Moses was given the power to judge and administer the people on the journey. When it came time for new leaders to take some of Moses's burden, the Sprit's power was taken and given to others. This was demonstrated with the new men prophesying.[291] The Spirit is very active in the Old Testament. The Spirit of the Lord was also seen as being poured out on specific individuals who would do the Lord's work.[292] This would lead to justice, righteousness, and peace for those around the person who had the Spirit.[293] It also resulted in the people committing their full devotion to the Lord.[294] The Spirit is promised to all believers in the Old Testament, but the time has not come for its fulfillment. This would all change with the coming Messiah. However, He would not come to all believers until Pentecost. His time to take the lead regarding working side by side with all Christians would not begin until Jesus sent Him.

The coming birth of Jesus also greatly increased the known work of the Holy Spirit. Just as John the Baptist was to be the forerunner of the Messiah, so also is the Holy Spirit preparing the way for His arrival. In Matthew 1, Mary was approached by a messenger from the Lord. He informed Mary that she was to be the mother of God and that through her son, the sins of the world would be forgiven. When

---

289 Dt. 7:1.
290 Dt. 8:19-20
291Nm. 11:25.
292 Is. 32:15.
293 Erickson, 792.
294 Is. 44:3-5. Ez. 36:26-28 also addresses this component of the Spirit.

she questioned how this could be, the angel responded that the Holy Spirit would conceive within her, Jesus, the Messiah. In Luke 1, we also have another child greatly influenced or filled by the Holy Spirit. John the Baptist, the relative of Jesus, was filled with the Holy Spirit in his mother, Elizabeth's womb, and leaped with the arrival of Mary and her unborn son, Jesus. Within this narrative, we have two unborn people filled with the Holy Spirit recognizing the presence of the other from within the womb.

Early in Jesus' ministry, a leading spiritual leader was presented with the good news that would be fulfilled in his day. John 3 is where Jesus, the Son, and Nicodemus, a member of the Sanhedrin, are discussing the power of God. Jesus is letting him know how the Spirit of God works. Nicodemus does not comprehend the life-sustaining nature of the Holy Spirit, nor does he see how the spiritual life is also sustained by the same Spirit. To be fair to Nicodemus, no one understood, outside of Jesus, how the Spirit would relate to the people. It will take faith for him, or anyone else, to see and experience the Holy Spirit's power, but if we miss the workings of the Spirit, all will be lost.

Another occurrence of the Holy Spirit at the start of Jesus' public ministry is at His baptism.[295] Holy Spirit descends on Jesus like a dove, and He is filled with His Spirit. The Father is well pleased and sends the Spirit to be with Jesus and guide Him in His earthly ministry. It is well documented that Jesus often went to pray with His Father, making the unified Trinity a priority.[296] Jesus also shows His followers how they are to be His disciples and follow His example in prayer and action. Even though it will be the Father and the Son sending the Holy Spirit in Acts, here Jesus is submitting to the role of the Holy Spirit. It says that the Spirit took Him to the wilderness for

---

295 Mt. 3
296 Mk, 1:35; 14:23; 6:46; Jn 6:15; Lk 6:12; 9:18

the forty days of testing.[297] "The Son follows the lead of the Spirit and performs miracles in the power of the Spirit; nevertheless, the Spirit knows that His authority is not permanent. . . . The Spirit assumes this authority over the incarnate Son and assists the Son in glorifying the Father."[298] The Spirit has several personal qualities that should be distinguished from the other two.

The first distinguishing part of the Holy Spirit's person is His sustaining of all life. Although the Holy Spirit sustains all of life, He only pours Himself into or fills His special creation of mankind once they have repented and made the Son, Lord of their lives. No other animal or object has the indwelling of the Spirit. He not only sustains but also builds a relationship with the believer. "Part of the Spirit's work is to hover over creation, keeping things intact. In this regard, we see the Spirit as the divine Preserver and Protector. . . The Spirit brings order out of disorder. He orders and preserves what God creates and redeems.[299] Going back to Genesis 1, we have the three persons of the Trinity saying Let us make man in our image.

The second distinguished action of the Holy Spirit is the close nature He will have with His role of helper. This was announced by Jesus in John 14. Here, Jesus is letting His disciples know that when I leave, I am not leaving you alone. I will not leave you as orphans.[300] Jesus used the word *paraclete* to give definition to both His relationship with the followers, but that of the Spirit as well. The *paraclete* in the "ancient world was someone summoned to give assistance in a court of law."[301] In the translation of this word, there are several options to be considered in English: comforter, counselor,

---

297 Mt. 4:1.
298 Ware, Father Son and Holy Spirit., 128.
299 Sproul, The Mysteries of the Holy Spirit,.71.
300 Jn. 14:18.
301 Sproul, Mysteries of the Holy Spirit, 148.

or helper. Many times, the translator will choose two of these definitions to describe one word. It should not be missed that the phrase, "and I will send "another" *paraclete.*"[302] This is making the point that Jesus was there to live beside them through His earthly ministry, but there is coming a day soon that He would leave them, but they were not to be discouraged because He would send another. Verses 16 and 17 state: the role of the Holy Spirit is about to change with people professing Christ as Lord. Jesus tells His disciples that all who believe in me will have the Holy Spirit and He will not depart from them.

It is at Pentecost that Acts 1:8 reveals the power of the Holy Spirit and is given to the new believers in Christ. Jesus had given some of the disciples the Holy Spirit when He breathed on them in John 20:22, but not all new believers had the Spirit before Pentecost. Thomas, for instance, was not with Jesus, and with his absence, he did not receive the Spirit until the upper room experience at Pentecost, where a mighty display of the Spirit's power was unveiled in Acts 2. Again, we see a mighty rushing wind/breath coming down to the people waiting for Him to come. The disciples need to see the "parallel between the Spirit's work in creation and redemption. As He is in the generating power of biological life, so He is the source and generating power of spiritual life."[303] The meaning of Pentecost has a great number of lessons as it pertains to the Holy Spirit. This is the first time He has shown His full power and direction for all believers. Pentecost is the birth of the new Church, and "Every Christian from Pentecost to the present is both regenerated of the Spirit and baptized in the Spirit. That is the essence of the meaning of Pentecost. Anything less casts a shadow over the sacred importance of Pentecost in the history of redemption. Any person who is regenerate is also sealed by the

---

302 Jn. 14:16.
303 Sproul, Mystery of the Holy Spirit. P.75

Spirit, baptized by the Spirit, and has the earnest of the Spirit."[304] Pentecost was the beginning of God moving with His people, and for the first time, the people of God did not have to worry about losing the Spirit. The Christians were charged with being disciples of Jesus and following His teachings with the help of the Holy Spirit.

Salvation comes from the Triune God and His word to the people. The Spirit is to work through the Bible and the gospel of Jesus Christ for the salvation of the sinner, and He does not work independently of this work.[305] The Old Testament book of Ezekiel states that the Holy Spirit will be given to man to make it possible to follow the will of God, and through this, man can seek and know God.[306] The promise of redemption is evident that this is a special occasion for man and Creator to be at one in spirit. The one who is following God had to be changed, and the ability and willingness to follow his teachings come from the Spirit. None of us is exempt, and this shows that the Spirit did not change roles when the New Covenant came into being.[307] The Spirit is still changing the hearts of the unbeliever to believers. Acts 26:18 likens our hardened hearts to be in the darkness, and the Holy Spirit is there to turn on the light, revealing God.

The Holy Spirit is the illuminator of the Bible, Jesus, and the Father. "At the ecumenical Council of Constantinople in A.D. 381, the church confessed and declared that the Holy Spirit is the 'Life-giver' (*Zoapoion*). The Spirit is the immediate source of all life."[308] 2 Tim 3:16 uses the word "breathed" as a reference that all Scripture is overseen by the Holy Spirit. It is His responsibility for illuminating the authors in their writing as well as the reader's interpreting the

---

304 Ibid, 132.
305 Ware, Father Son, Holy Spirit, 119.
306 Ez. 36:26-27.
307 Eph. 2:1.
308 Sproul, Mystery of the Holy Spirit, 73.

word. The Spirit is the keeper of the very word of God. Just as He sustains mortal life, He sustains our eternal life.

Even with knowing that the Spirit gives us a new heart, convicts us of sin, and protects our salvation, it must be understood that "the Spirit, then, does not work in an independent saving manner apart from the proclamation and knowledge of the gospel of Christ, for it is only by the knowledge of this gospel that any can be saved. Since the Spirit has come to glorify Jesus."[309] So what is the work of the Spirit in salvation? "The Holy Spirit is the Sanctifier. He is the One who applies the work of Christ to our lives by working in us to bring us to full conformity and the image of Christ. The goal of redemption is holiness."[310] Jesus is on His way to heaven so that the Holy Spirit can do His job of convicting sin and sanctifying the new believer.[311] Jesus is concluding His mission of giving the good news and providing a sacrifice for our sins, but only through His going away will the Holy Spirit come and give the power of sanctification and conviction to the people. The Father is Holy, and as judge, we are to be made holy like He is holy.[312] The only possible way for this to happen is to believe that the Son has taken your sins upon Himself, and the Holy Spirit changes your heart and begins the sanctification process.

Sanctification is not a task anyone can do on their own. While people are still on a sin-stained planet, there will always be a struggle to live a godly life. This is why the Father and the Son sent the Holy Spirit. The original *Paraclete* was Jesus, and His admonition to Nicodemus was that he needed to be born again.[313] This new birth was

---

[309] Ware, Father, Son, and Holy Spirit, 117,
310 Sproul, Mystery of the Holy Spirit, 95.
310 Ibid, 95
311 Jn. 16:7-14.
312 1 Pt. 1:16-17.
313 Jn. 3:3.

to be a spiritual birth that shows our transformation and new life in the Spirit. Going back to John 3 with Jesus and Nicodemus, Jesus shares that the Spirit is like the wind. He cannot be seen, but the actions of the Spirit are evident. He clarifies to him that a person must be born of the Spirit to be saved and considered born again.[314] Later in John 6:46-49, Jesus is instructing His followers that they will have to drink His blood and eat His flesh to live with Him in heaven. Who would advocate that we become cannibals and follow Him? The great crowd dispersed, and many stopped following, thinking that this kind of teaching was too hard to understand. He tells His remaining followers that without the Spirit, there is no life and no real understanding of spiritual matters. Man in his own state cannot understand the correct teachings of Jesus, and this is the cause of the multitude falling away. He states in John 6:60-71 that His words and teachings cannot be understood outside of the Spirit. Jesus even questioned the twelve on their loyalty and desire to stay, but even as they were saying, "What other option do we have?" He assures them that He knows who will stay and who will not. He even informs them that there are some who will continue to follow but will not be there in the end. We can only be children of God if the Spirit makes it happen.

When discussing sanctification, we must look at the process of how the Spirit keeps the children of God. Jesus assures His disciples that there will be another, *paraclete,* who will come and be with them while Jesus goes to prepare a place for them. The Spirit will convict the world of sin, righteousness, and judgment.[315] The Spirit will also guide them in all truth. He will not be here to give a new word but will give the words of Jesus and glorify the Son, just as the Son will glorify the Father.

---

314 Jn. 3:8.
315 Jn. 16:7

The New Covenant will establish a sealing of the Spirit.[316] In the Old Covenant, the Spirit would reside with specific leaders as long as they were holding up their end of the covenant agreement. So when Saul sacrificed without Samuel, the Spirit left him.[317] Now the Spirit will have a permanent residence with the Christian. The Spirit will be with the individual person, because each person accepting the salvation gift of the Son will be the temple of the Holy Spirit. The people no longer need to travel to the temple to worship. They are the temple.[318] The Spirit is responsible to seal those who have been chosen and partake in the salvation of Christ.[319] Eph 1:8 is where Paul tells his readers that the implied giver of wisdom from John is giving wisdom to those chosen for salvation. "When you heard the message of truth, the gospel of your salvation, and when you believed in Him, you were also sealed with the promised Holy Spirit."[320] There must be a hearing of the word, and our responsibility is to present the word for others to make the decision to accept or reject Christ. The disciples did not save anyone, and the disciples do not keep the convert secure. The disciple's job is to tell, and the Holy Spirit will do the rest.

The power of the Holy Spirit is most visibly evident in Acts 1. Here, the Spirit is described as being like a rushing wind and a flame of fire falling down on the new Christian community. The power demonstrated made the new Christians bold for their new faith and determined to spread the gospel of Jesus, no matter the cost. The Greek word for power is □□□□□□□□□dunamin□□This word picture of the Holy Spirit was so strong that starting in□1867, the Swedish word *dynamite* was coined by the Swedish chemist Alfred

---

316 Eph. 1:13-14.
317 1 Sm. 16:14.
318 1 Cor. 6:19-20.
319 Eph. 1:4.
320 Eph. 1:13 (HCSB)

Nobel to describe the power of his new invention, dynamite. [321] The ever-present power of the Spirit was what he equated with the power of this new invention that moved mountains. The Holy Spirit's power goes beyond all the dynamite we could string together, for He truly is all-powerful.

The Holy Spirit is full of power and is the conquering force for our salvation and life in Christ. The Christian, however, is not able to do anything on his own. To be apart from the Holy Spirit is to be apart from the Son. Romans 8:6 carefully states that on our own, man will be dead. It later states that life with the Spirit brings life and peace. The Christian is also helped by the Spirit in the spiritual disciplines. The Spirit is there to help in prayer. Praying to the Father in the Son's name is the proper way to pray, but there will be times when the Christian is lacking in words or wisdom. As in the paragraph above, we are to be as one with the Father as the Son is with the Father, but our understanding of who He is has escaped our understanding, and man's vulnerability is expressed with silence. This is where the Holy Spirit takes man's thoughts and verbalizes God's desires to the Son for the Father. (Romans 8:26) This is where we get to pray to the Father, in the name of the Son and in the power of the Holy Spirit. Without the Spirit helping man, there would be no ability to pray with any effect.

Another important word to discuss when studying the Holy Spirit is ☐☐☐☐☐☐☐☐☐☐☐upernikomen☐☐☐In Romans 8:37, it takes three words to translate this one word. A translation of "more than conquerors" is often used for this single word. The prefix of *huper* comes across as the English word hyper. Paul is asserting that we are not just conquerors but hyper conquerors.[322] Romans 8:12-17

321 Dan McCormack, "dynamite" http://www.etymonline.com/index. php?term=dynamite (accessed April 18, 2017)

322 Sproul, The Mystery of the Holy Spirit, 38.

lets the Christian know that the Spirit not only lets us win in Spiritual battles with His power, but it is through the Spirit that Christians can be given the distinct title of a child of God. It is through His testimony that He is transforming us to the likeness of the Son. He is always in likeness of the Father. The Holy Spirit helps the Christian accomplish this task.

The Spirit is also the one who will be the judge of the ruler of the world, Satan.[323] The road ahead for the followers of Christ will not be easy because Satan and sin are here to slow the Christian down, but this is why He sends the Spirit. Later in chapter sixteen, John tells of Jesus' teaching on the peace He will bring through the Spirit because of the upcoming suffering they will have to endure, but "Be courageous! I have conquered the world."[324]

The Holy Spirit has the task of equipping the saints for ministry. "In God's plan of redemption, the Holy Spirit has gifted every believer for ministry. The whole church has been empowered from on high."[325] Just as He helps with prayer, the Holy Spirit helps with daily life and ministry work. He does not empower every believer to do the same ministry, so each person is uniquely equipped to do his ministry as the Spirit directs. It is through the Spirit that all the parts of the body of the Church are placed together.[326] It is the Spirit's role to give out the gifts to each member. The members are to function where they are gifted and not try to do another Christian's job. The member should seek to increase their giftings. Following is a list of some of the gifts given: apostles, prophets, teachers, miracles, healing, helping, managing, and various languages.[327] The gift or gifts given need to be

---

323 Jn 16:11.
324 Jn 16:33 (HCSB).
325 Sproul, The Mystery of the Holy Spirit, 131.
326 1 Co. 12:13.
327 1 Co. 12:27.

tended to by their recipients. Paul reminds Timothy in his second letter to fan into flame the gift that is in you from the laying on of my hands.[328] This passage indicates that there was a special gift given to Timothy during his ordination. In Exodus 35:30-35, it is the Spirit of God who fills Bezalel and Oholiab with the gifts of wisdom, understanding, and ability to do all the work required for the making of the tabernacle. Then, as leaders, they were led by the Spirit to work with other gifted workers to accomplish the task. The workers that were chosen by the Holy Spirit were given the gift of wisdom and then the talent to complete the work.

It is often missed that anything that is lasting must first be directed by God. The workers with Bezalel were already talented people and could make part of the tents by their naturally God given gifts. The Holy Spirit, however, was the one who chose to give the men a special ability to complete the project according to God's desire. He specially gifted them to complete the work. The most interesting fact is that the most important gift given was wisdom. It was the first gift mentioned in the passage and seems to be more important than ability.[329] It should also be noted that no one gets all the gifts. In 2 Timothy, Paul tells Timothy that he, Paul, was gifted as a herald, apostle, and teacher, and then he mentions again to guard the good things in the power of the Holy Spirit. The Spirit is there to help in all aspects of our everyday life.[330] By walking in the Spirit, you will do the things of God. If you are not walking with Him, you will do the will of the flesh, for it is only in the power of the Spirit that we can succeed in spiritual things.

Galatians 5 says that it will be clear when you are not close to the Spirit. You can observe when people choose not to follow the Spirit by their actions. They will be involved with sexual relations outside

---

328 2 Tim. 1:6.
329 Ex. 36
330 Gl. 5:16.

of marriage; they will make bad moral choices that will affect others. There will be multiple issues with putting other things before God. The people will not allow the Spirit to direct any decision. There will be hurt feelings, and a feeling of self-importance will destroy close relationships, and a desire to have what everyone else possesses will be high.[331]

Conversely, the fruit of the Spirit is love, joy, peace, patience, kindness, goodness, faith, gentleness, self-control."[332] You can be nice to others, and you can be a great speaker, but without the fruit of the Spirit, you are not His. Only the Spirit can give the fruit of the Spirit. Just like apple trees can only bear apples, so only those alive in the Spirit can have true joy. This is a natural outcome for those who have the Spirit within. It can also be noted that this is not a collection of different fruits, but a singular fruit. The □□, os, ending in Greek on the word fruit indicates that even though we have a list of descriptors, it is a single entity. Love is not to be separated from joy. They all need to be present for the fruit to be correct and from the Spirit. The first word used to define the fruit is *agape.* The meaning of this love was discussed earlier as the ultimate love only God can give. We love Him because He first loved us.[333] This definition of "love" can only come from God; therefore, we can only bear the fruit of the Holy Spirit if He is in our lives. All of these descriptive words for the fruit of the Spirit are inverses of the works of the flesh. Everyone who is a Christian must produce spiritual fruit.

The Holy Spirit is also tasked with appointing prophets, judges, and kings. He is also the one who set aside the missionaries who went with Paul. Even with all the things mentioned above, His largest role has been the life-giver to all humanity. He is the one who sustains us

---

331 Gl. 5:19-21.
332 Gl. 6:22-23 (HCSB).
333 1 Jn. 4:19.

each day. He is also the one who raised Jesus from the dead, according to Romans 8:11.[334] As the person who sustains life, it is fitting that the description of the Spirit being the breath of God would be used to show the power of life in humanity. The Father breathed into man to make him alive in Genesis 1. Jesus breathed the Holy Spirit on the disciples after His death and gave Spiritual life to the believers at the end of John. The Christian must be careful in understanding the Holy Spirit and His role in the Trinity lest we get off course.

It is easy to see that the third person of the Trinity takes a subordinate role to the Father and the Son. It should also be noted that His equality is not to be questioned. However, over the years, many well-intentioned people have desired to elevate the Holy Spirit to an unnatural position in the Trinity. In so doing, they have created a new movement, glossolalia. This is a twentieth-century movement that added speaking in an angelic language as a major part of the worship service. In John MacArthur's book, *Strange Fire,* he lays out several concerns he has for this new movement and how he believes it can greatly hurt the advancement of the universal church. He states, "Any affirmation of modern glossolalia- even if it is relegated only to the prayer closet- encourages believers to seek deeper spiritual intimacy with God through mystical, muddled, and even mindless experiences. This is a dangerous practice for believers, who are called to renew their minds, not bypass their intellectual faculties or subjugate reason to raw emotion. Any emphasis on tongues can also foster spiritual pride in the church."[335] Many in the charismatic and holiness churches have placed this special emphasis on the Holy Spirit. Many from these groups would even say that speaking in heavenly words is a proof of salvation, but many like MacArthur believe that some gifts have stopped with the spread of the gospel to the far reaches of the earth.

---

334 Sproul, The Mystery of the Holy Spirit, 25.
335 John MacArthur, Strange Fire. (Nashville: Thomas Nelson, 2013), 244.

Then speaking multiple languages, such as in Acts with Peter at Pentecost, is a viable usage of a continued gift.[336] The person of the Holy Spirit does not need our help because some people think He has been given a lesser job within the Trinity. Rather, we need to worship and understand each of the persons in their individual responsibilities and functions located in the Trinity.

The last person of the Trinity is the Holy Spirit. The Spirit is Coequal in majesty but subordinate in function.[337] It is in His function that we learn about His person. The personhood of the Spirit is described by the Son to be masculine, despite the neuter function of the word for Spirit. He is to be respected as a person and deserves our obedience. He is the person of the Trinity who sustains all life and brings us power to do His will. Within the New Covenant, He is the sealer of our souls, guide, and comforter in our mortal bodies. In our immortal bodies, He is here to help sanctify us for eternity. His personal power has been demonstrated for the world to see, and through this power, we are led to conviction and salvation from our sin. Through the work of the Trinity, He has conquered evil. He then grants gifts to the believers for service, calls men to serve, and all Christians will see the fruit of His Spirit in their lives.

---

336 Ibid, 244.
337 Grudem, p.253

CONCLUSION

The Trinity is a multi-faceted and complex thought that takes a great deal of time to study, and we may never be able to fully understand Him here or in heaven. That is why we call it a mystery. The Old Testament person only viewed God as a singular being, at most a Father God with an active Spirit that is not separate. A single person without the complication of multiplicity, because He declared, I am one, and there is no other.[338] The One in essence of God was such a tight-knit thought that man did not even look for another person, just the essence. When the Spirit of God was seen in the Old Testament, it would not be out of place because everyone accepted that God was Spirit. The real dilemma came about with the New Testament's introduction of Jesus. The promised Messiah was much more than a person coming to save the people from an occupying army or invading force. He was claiming to be God. How could this be? There is to be one God, and this man claims to be the great I Am.[339] Then, as the Son was about to leave, He promised to send the Holy Spirit. The Spirit was to seal the hearts of men and be God with the people. All are monotheistic, yet they all claim to be the one, God.

The early church had a real problem with placing into words the essence of God as being one, and yet there are three distinguished persons of the essence. The essence of God is who or what makes up a being. Plato's philosophic arguments that were made before the birth of Jesus used three distinctive words defined below. These definitions

---

338 Dt 6:9.
339 John 8:48-49

are of great importance for the church Fathers. It gave them a valid explanation of their beliefs. Plato introduced three words that explained how the three persons do not go against the law of non-contradiction with the one in essence. The "existence" of something means that something is real and changing. All people exist is a correct statement. Everyone goes about life in an ever-changing world, and change is consistent because people exist in time. Every millisecond changes our age. You cannot remove your foot from the same river you placed it in because the river has changed since you first put it in. With this explanation, one can surmise that God does not exist. He is not changing, and He is not bound by time. He is, however, "essence". This is the unmoving, unchangeable, constant that is over the whole. It is the essence that defines Him as a being, and as a being, He is known as God. No matter what one believes concerning our origins, one must believe in something outside of time and space that started everything. God, the creator, by definition must be outside of time and space and is not changing. In His essence, He sets the laws, makes the rules, and becomes the very definition of words like love. The third word is "subsistence" or under being. This is where the persons of the Trinity are defined. This definition is what the church fathers used: the Holy Spirit is co-equal in majesty, but subordinate in function.[340] The Holy Spirit here is stating that He is one with the essence, but when it comes to His person, He is willing to be subordinate to the other Persons. He takes on special roles and works in lockstep with the other two persons for all tasks to be perfectly completed.

The next section must address the question of who can rightfully claim to be God. If I tell you my wife has brown hair and hazel eyes. Then, as different women enter the room, all claiming to be my wife, you have some evidence to disregard many of them due to their

---

340 R.C. Sproul, Who is the Holy Spirit, (Sanford, FL: Reformation Trust, 2012), .5-9.

descriptions. You can see that those who are blonde would be disqualified. If a lady comes into the room and has brown hair, that does not automatically make her my wife. It calls for further investigation. Does she also have hazel eyes? If not, then she cannot be my wife. Even if she does, it calls for more investigation. Only when all the characteristics are covered and I come and identify her will you begin to believe she is my wife. You will then see how we relate to each other and so on. So when we turn to God, we must ask the same kinds of questions. Who has the authority to be called God, and does that Person tell the reader that others should be eliminated from consideration? Starting with the Father, it has been established that He possesses the attributes of God and He accepts these claims. He also connects His work with the Son and Spirit that He embraces them as God as well. He in no way claims that they are not God, and yet He claims that there is but one God to serve. Having observed that He holds all the characteristics of God, we will observe the evidence and allow Him to share with us His essence.

The Son is to be examined next. He also accepts worship from men and tells His followers that He is the way to the Father in John 14. In this same chapter, He does not eliminate the Father or the Spirit from being God. He claims that the Father and He are one, and no one can have one without the other. To top it off, He also said that the Father and the Son will be sending the Holy Spirit, who is going to be with the people. In all of this, He never gives up the claim that there is one God to be worshiped.

The Holy Spirit is the last manifestation of God to be discussed in His being. He may be the last mentioned in the study, and He may be the last name used in the baptismal story, but He has been from before the beginning of time. He was also very active in the creation of the universe. The Spirit does meet the qualifications of being God and accepts worship, but He is always seen as one who points to the

Son.[341] Although He is God, He will always point to the others, and He will acknowledge their deity, yet He will testify there is but one God. We have also observed His actions as being all powerful, and He has the witness of the Son.

This conundrum has led us straight to the mystery of the Trinity. Looking at the philosophical arguments, there are just some things not understood, but that does not mean there is no answer. How do we fight infection? Today, we give antibiotics that will kill the bacteria in our bodies. The great mystery was revealed by Alexander Fleming in his bacterial lab. Even if it was a mistake, a mystery was solved.[342] Just because one side does not yet comprehend does not make the argument false. It simply means that the other side does understand the argument at this point, and even if man never understands, God the Author knows.

The next logical step is for the great thinkers of the past to see how they have wrestled with this topic. It was established that this argument is full of pitfalls and misunderstandings as a philosophical argument. From the first century's defining arguments, these men helped the church begin the work on this monumental doctrine. It seemed that the moment someone was willing to place their words in writing, a fatal flaw was found in the argument. On occasion, it also caused a crisis of belief and teaching. There were many centuries where the people were content with the previous church fathers' teachings and left the argument alone in peace. However, there have been a handful of very contentious years where heresies were tried before great counsels. Modalism, Partialism, and Arianism were all condemned through the years. Trinitarian doctrines are also found in the arguments of who sent the Holy Spirit. The Eastern and Western

---

341 Jn 15:26.
342_____ . "Alexander Fleming a Biography". https://www.biography.com/people/alexander-fleming-9296894? (accessed July 26, 2017).

churches split over this argument and have never been unified again. It is also seen that part of the protestant reformation was a result of how the Trinity works in the Lord's Supper. The view of transubstantiation turned into four views, and many denominations have not agreed and defined their own beliefs.

The last part of the research comes in the form of the Persons of God. If God is one in essence and there are three Persons in subsistence of the essence, then what distinguishes them and their roles? The role of the Father is seen as the grand architect who has all the plans for creation and what will happen with it. He takes the lead in having all the glory and is the one sitting on the throne of heaven. He shows Himself as a father and gives people the correct relationship a father is to have with his son. He was so close to His Son that Jesus said, "If you know me, you know my Father."[343] He will show man all he needs to do to live as a Father.

The Son is before time, and His appearance as a man truly shows people how they are to live. "Follow me" is what He told His disciples. This short section only covered one of the four gospels, John. Jesus was the sacrifice for the people's sins. He is now at the right hand of the Father. He shows us that when you pray to the Father, you must pray in the name of the Son. The Son is the mediator of man to the Father. There is no skipping Jesus, the Son, to get into heaven. He walked with the people and was a *paraclete* to them in their life's journey. He would send the Holy Spirit in Acts 1 to comfort the people and be with them wherever they were as He left His earthly presence. It is on Jesus that all power and authority are placed in heaven and on earth.[344] He was the perfect man and perfect sacrifice for all who

---

343 Jn 14:7 (HCSB).
344 Mt. 28.

accept His name and His work.[345] His job was also to reflect His glory back to the Father.

In sending the Holy Spirit, Jesus made a way for all humanity to have God with them. The Holy Spirit seals for salvation; he is there to give the believer words for prayer. He is to be the one who gives power when we pray. In addition to this, the Holy Spirit is there to ensure that the Father and Son receive the glory due to them. If Christians follow the example of Biblical worship, we will be led by the Spirit to worship the Father and Son in the Spirit. Just as the Holy Spirit was with Jesus, He is with those who profess Jesus as Lord and Savior. It is the Holy Spirit that seals us for salvation. It is also to the Spirit that no one should ever lie to or quench His work. The Son said that the worst sin possible was to go blaspheme the Holy Spirit, and this is even worse than blaspheming the Son.[346]

There can be no doubt that the subject of the Trinity is not an easy topic to understand, but through using the Bible and looking at other scholars, it can be seen that God truly wants to know His creation. He sets the example of cooperation, relationships, worship, and prayer. Christianity is the only religion that espouses the notion that the supreme creator and ruler of the universe desires to have a special relationship with each human. There is a way to have a perfect relationship with the Father. There is a perfect sacrifice in Jesus as Savior and Lord of your life. There is a way to know that God will never leave you and provides for your spiritual power through the Holy Spirit. All of this happens with just one God. Never stop the pursuit of God, because He wants you to know Him. "Listen, Israel: The Lord is our God, the Lord is one. Love the Lord your God with all your heart, with all your soul, and with all your strength. These words that I am giving you today are to be in your heart. Repeat them

---

345 Jn 3:16.
346 Mk 3:29

to your children. Talk about them when you sit in your house and when you walk along the road, when you lie down and when you get up."[347]

347 Dt. 6:4-8 (HCSB).

BIBLIOGRAPHY

2022. In *Merriam-Webster.com*. Retrieved Dec. 9, 2022, from https://www.merriam-webster.com/dictionary/ "Alexander Fleming a Biography".

https://www.biography.com/people/alexander-fleming-9296894? (accessed July 26, 2017).

"Cancer Vaccines and Their Side Effects." *American Cancer Society*. https://www.cancer.org/treatment/treatments-and-side-effects/treatment-types/immunotherapy/cancer-vaccines.html. Accessed 12/9/2022.

"History of Astronomy." Britannica.

https://www.britannica.com/science/astronomy/History-of-astronomy. Accessed 12/9/2022.

"James Webb Helps Clarify the Number of Galaxies in the Universe." *The Universe*

Space Tech. https://universemagazine.com/en/james-webb-helps-clarify-the-number-of-galaxies-in-the-universe/. Accessed 12/9/2022.

_____ Systematic Theology: An Introduction to Biblical Doctrine. Grand Rapids: Zondervan, 1994.

Akin, Daniel L. *A Theology for the Church.* Nashville: B & H Publishing Group, 2007.

Allison, Gregg R. Historical Theology: An Introduction to Christian Doctrine. Grand Rapids:

Zondervan, 2011.

Begg, Alistair and Sinclair Ferguson. *Name Above all Names.* Wheaton: Crossway, 2013.

Blankenhorn, David. *Fatherless America.* New York: Basic Books, 1995.

Davies, Paul. "The Secret of Life Won't Be Cooked Up in a Chemistry Lab." *Guardian:*

January 13, 2013.

Elwell, Walter, ed. *Evangelical Dictionary of Theology* . 2nd. Grand Rapids: Baker Academic, 2001.

Erickson, Millard, J. *Christian Theology: Third edition*. Grand Rapids: Baker Books, 2013

Ford, LeRoy. Design for Teaching and Training: A Self-Study Guide to Lesson Planning.

Nashville: Broadman Press, 1978.

Geisler, Norman. *Systematic Theology.* Vol. 2. 3 vols. Minneapolis: Bethany House, 2003.

George, Timothy and Denise. Ed., Baptist Confessions, Covenants, and Catechisms. Nashville:

B&H Books, 1996

Gonzalez, Justo L. *The Story of Christianity.* Vol. 2. New York: Harper Collins, 1984.

—--. *The Story of Christianity Vol.1.* New York: Harper-Collins, 1984

Guralnik, David B. Websters: New World Dictionary of the American Language. Cleveland:

William Collins, 1980

Grogan, Geoffery W. The Expositor's Bible Commentary: Isaiah, Jeremiah, Lamentations,

Ezekiel. ed.by Frank E. Gaebelein. Grand Rapids: Zondervan, 1986.

Grudem, Wayne. *Systematic Theology.* Grand Rapids: Zondervan, 1994.

Hemphill, Ken. *The Prayer of Jesus.* Nashville: Broadman and Holman, 2001.

Hildebrand, Stephen, trans. *On the Holy Spirit.* Yonkers, New York: St Vladimir's Seminary Press, 2011.

House, Paul R. *Bonhoeffer's Seminary Vision.* Wheaton: Crossway, 2015.

House, Wayne H. *Charts of Christian Theology and Doctrine*: Zondervan, Nashville, 1992.

James, Stephen and David Thomas. *Wild Things: The Art of Nurturing Boys.* Carol Stream, IL:

Tyndale, 2009

Jowdy, Laura, C.A. Archivist & Collections Manager, Congressional Medal of Honor Society.

Medal of Honor a Primer.
https://www.cmohs.org/media/24881.pdf/view. May 2019.

Accessed December 12, 2022.

Lewis, C. S. *The Last Battle.* New York: Macmillan Company, 1970.

MacArthur, John. *Strange Fire*. Nashville: Thomas Nelson, 2013.

Mason, Eric. *Manhood Restored.* Nashville: B&H Publishing Group, 2013.

McCormack, Dan. "Dynamite"
http://www.etymonline.com/index.php?term=dynamite.

accessed April 18, 2017.

Mohler, Albert, Jr. "The Gospel According to Jesus - 20 Years Later." *albertmohler.com*, June 2008.

Mohler, R. Albert. "The Shack-The Missing Art of Evangelical Discernment" *R. Albert Mohler*

Blog. www.albertmohler.com/2010/01/27the-shack-the-missing-art-of-evangelical-discernment, Accessed March 29, 2017.

Reid Patton, "Fathers Do Not Embitter Your Children", *Journey on Today. June 29, 2016.*

http://brentwoodbaptist.com/journeyon-today/2016-06-29/ (accessed March 14, 2017).

Pearcey, Nancy. *Finding Truth.* Colorado Springs: David C. Cook, 2015.

Robertson, Archibald T. Word Pictures in the New Testament: Vol 4 The Fourth Gospel, The

Epistle to the Hebrews. Nashville: Broadman Press, 1960

Schreiner, Thomas and Matthew Crawford. *The Lord's Supper,* Nashville: B&H Printing, 2010.

Scott, Frank W. The Preacher's Complete Homiletic Commentary: On the Gospel According to

John, Grand Rapids: Baker Books, 1996.

Sproul, R.C. *The Mystery of the Holy Spirit*. Ross Shire, Scotland: Christian Focus, 2011.

Sproul, R. C. "Mystery of the Trinity." *Ligonier Ministries.* Orlando:

https://www.ligonier.org/learn/series/mystery-of-the-trinity. Accessed 12/9/2022.

Sproul, R.C. *Who is the Holy Spirit.* Sanford, FL: Reformation Trust, 2012.

Stein, Robert. "Fatherhood of God."

http://www.biblestudytools.com/dictionaries/bakers-evangelical-dictionary/fatherhood-of-god.htm, Accessed August 8, 2016.

Tenney, Merril. *The Expositor's Bible Commentary vol. 9.* Grand Rapids: Zondervan, 1981.

Unger, Merrill F. *The New Unger's Bible Dictionary.* Chicago: Moody Press, 1988.

Ware, Bruce. Father, Son, and Holy Spirit: Relationships, Roles, and Relevance. Wheaton: Crossway, 2005.

Ware, Bruce A. *The Man Christ Jesus.* Wheaton: Crossway, 2013.

Ware, Bruce, Keith Goad, Tyler Wittman, Matt Wireman and Chad Brand. "The SBJT Forum: God the Holy Spirit." *The Southern Baptist Journal of Theology* 16.4 (2012): 96-105.

Wolfendale, James. The Preacher's Complete Homiletic Commentary on the Fifth Book of

Moses Called Deuteronomy. Grand Rapids: Baker Books, 1996.

www.ingramcontent.com/pod-product-compliance
Lightning Source LLC
LaVergne TN
LVHW022323080426
835508LV00041B/2167